half pants full pants

REAL-LIFE TALES FROM SHIMOGA

ANAND SUSPI

INDIA • SINGAPORE • MALAYSIA

Copyright © Anand Subbarao 2022
All Rights Reserved.

ISBN 979-8-88849-610-7

This book has been published with all efforts taken to make the material error-free after the consent of the author. However, the author and the publisher do not assume and hereby disclaim any liability to any party for any loss, damage, or disruption caused by errors or omissions, whether such errors or omissions result from negligence, accident, or any other cause.

While every effort has been made to avoid any mistake or omission, this publication is being sold on the condition and understanding that neither the author nor the publishers or printers would be liable in any manner to any person by reason of any mistake or omission in this publication or for any action taken or omitted to be taken or advice rendered or accepted on the basis of this work. For any defect in printing or binding the publishers will be liable only to replace the defective copy by another copy of this work then available.

To Dinky and Noodle

· · · · · · · · ● ● ● ● · · · · · · ·

In my belief, most of us continually move in
two opposite directions.
While we plan our future and dream about it,
we also peer backwards and re-live our past.
Nostalgia is one of the most underrated but
overindulged themes of mankind.

· · · · · · · · ● ● ● ● · · · · · ·

FOREWORD

Thank you Suspi for bringing back the glory of childhood in the pre-internet days. It's a jolt book for many parents who strive to give their child a better life than they had: parents who have interpreted their fantastic childhood as being insufficient and quite shameful when viewed from the balcony of today. It's a fantasy book for today's children who are already more adult than the adults around them. This may kindle their license to be naive, stupid, innocent and sublimely ridiculous. It's a book that may remind some of us of our 'most happy' days. And some of us of the days we have tried so hard to forget.

Whatever it does to you, blame it all on the child who has been masquerading as a grown up for years. If you know Suspi, he is just waiting for a magic wand that will shrink him so that he can fit into a tiny pair of half pants or full pants and experience total chaos without knowing what it means. Very few people keep their childhood alive and fresh through the stupidities of adulthood. Suspi is one of a rare species. I have read the manuscript many times and each time I have come up with a new way to describe it.

For marketing and advertising folks who pride on strategy as if they have plotted the future course of other people's minds, it's a gentle reminder of what they are missing: the persuasive power of innocence. For authors who revel in the deeper meaning of life, it's a reminder of the pleasure of shallowness. For adults who like clicking selfies, the pages that follow may show them how beautiful life once was. And for those who have stopped reading books, I just feel sorry. They have just lost a chance to laugh at themselves. Lucky you, Suspi.

- R Balki

THIS HAS TO BE SAID

I am a first-time parent. As is the case with quite a few, this was unplanned. Let me term it as a `happy accident'. On a peaceful Sunday morning in 2012, I set out to write a page of prose in order to convince myself that I can write beyond advertising, and ended up with this collection of childhood memories. They are not different from yours. In fact, they are uncannily similar to what most children in the world grow up with. The only difference would be the names of the places and people. That's the gloriousness of childhood.

From conception to delivery, it's been a long journey of anticipation and at times, impatience. Through this, a large bunch of friends and well-wishers have maintained much enthusiasm on my behalf (for a debut author, this is oxygen.) Quite a few have made invaluable contributions without whom or which, this book would not be on the shelves today. You ought to know the people I love, admire and am grateful to.

Not many of us manage to stave off the complexities of today, more so the corporate world. About a year ago, I was fortunate enough to meet the exceptions at Hector Beverages. They read all of two stories and said, *"These take us back to a place in time that's innocent and charming. We want more people to experience the same. We will publish this book."* I cannot thank them enough for their instinctive patronage and uncommon perspective. While the world is trundling forward at a pace that we cannot handle sensibly, they are chugging backward into a world of simplicity and joy. There's no bigger testament to this than their brand, Paper Boat.

Months before I met them, while on a family holiday in Kashmir, Phalgun Tiruvasu suggested that I approach Paper Boat since the brand was all about nostalgia and so was the book. The fact that he was four drinks down and that this manuscript had been rejected by nearly ten publishing houses, possibly led to this `Eureka!' moment. Thank you Phala, for the most befitting idea for this book.

Balki has been my big boss for the longest stretch of my work life. That it was Bruce Lee in my growing up years is a different matter altogether. Balki does not indulge anyone or any piece of work if it does not tickle the `Balki Gut'. This book managed to do that, and that alone has given me immeasurable joy and energy. For thousands of people who have worked closely with him, his conviction and point of view mean the world. It would not be an exaggeration to say that he has been the most ardent fan of these stories.

Arun Raman, a very dear friend thought of the title for this book, over a drink. I need to buy him many more even if I never write another.

Harpal is my business partner, a wonderful designer and a great person. He was always my only choice to design the book cover. He will also be my only choice to design my tombstone, if I decide on having one.

Abhijit Bhaduri is many things rolled into one: an HR practitioner par excellence, speaker, columnist, author and cartoonist. To me, he's been an encouragement since I started working. He has guided me through various aspects of this novel.

Devi Yesodharan took upon the task of editing this book though her hands were full with work. Her skill and suggestions have added enormously to make this book worthy of being published. Else, the ineptness of writing would have jolted you on many a page.

Amit Monteiro and Amulya at Paper Boat went out of their way to figure out the process of publishing while being caught up in their regular marketing jobs. They did it displaying much ease and equanimity. I think the culture at Paper Boat has a lot to do with it.

Several people have made significant contributions in their own ways. Many have regularly followed up on the progress or the lack of it. Some have displayed disappointment and angst at my slackness and inability to get things going, and have come back with ideas, suggestions and connections to make this book see the light of day.

My sincere thanks to Adarsh, Aditi Chaudhuri, Ajoy Krishna, Anjana Pawar, Anshdeep, Archana Nagpal, Deepak Shetty, Elvis Sequeira, Nomit Joshi, Rachna Kalra, Rahul Sengupta, Rakhi Chaudhuri, Shagun Seda, Sudhir Makhija, Uma Nair, Vishak Acharya and Yogi Vashishta.

I cannot sign off without thanking my mom and dad (he passed away in 2009) and all my friends in Shimoga for making my childhood as memorable as childhood can be.

CONTENTS

PART 1: HALF PANT TALES FROM SHIMOGA

SHIMOGA

It was a small, sleepy town like any other. It wasn't so small that a prayer call from one mosque could be heard all over. But it wasn't too big either. Once, when someone stole a pant piece from a shop on Nehru Road and was promptly caught, most of the town heard about the incident within half an hour. The thief was beaten up badly. Some people in Shimoga thought he deserved it. Others felt that for a ten paise crime, he had been given three rupees of punishment. So, it wasn't really a sleepy town, thinking-and-conscience-wise. Shimoga had lots of doctors, engineers, teachers, schools and colleges, sugarcane and rice fields, coconut and arecanut trees, sandalwood, donkeys, cows and pigs, temples, cinema halls and *pani-puri* carts. It had one Nehru Road, one Nehru Stadium and one Gandhi Park. It also had an *Ajji* Field (Grandmother's Field) and to this day, no one knows why it was called that. Therefore, it also had an air of mystery.

The original name of the town is Shivamogga, meaning Shiva's Face. But everyone calls it Shimoga as it is easier on the mind and the tongue. Situated at the mouth of the pretty Malnad region, 274 km from Bangalore, it is the district capital but given its nature, I prefer to call it the district captain. It didn't draw any attention to itself but gave opportunities and played up the rest of the team around it. Just 18 km away is Bhadravati, the birthplace of Gundappa Vishwanath. This industrial hub boasted of a sugar factory, the Visweshwaraiyya Iron & Steel Plant, Mysore Paper Mills and other facilities of repute. Barely 96 km away in one direction is Jog Falls, India's highest waterfall. You come across the Agumbe Ghats if you head in a different direction. The Linganamakki Dam is also close by, as are the Kudremukha Iron Ore Mines, Kodachadri Hills, Gajnur Dam, Sringeri, and Kemmanagundi, all places of great pristine beauty. I hope this gives you a sense of the bigness of this small town. I'll now move on to the real big things about Shimoga.

The legendary super cop of Karnataka, S P Sangliana was posted here in my childhood. When his wife borrowed his office car to buy vegetables, he booked a case against her. So goes the legend. When the Chief Minister's car committed a traffic violation, he had it seized. His daughter, the only north eastern girl in class, studied with me in LKG.

(Standing in the top row exactly in the centre is S P Sangliana's daughter. I am on the extreme left in the second row from the top.)

When we had to put up the `Snow White' play, the nuns didn't waste a minute deciding who would play the main part. A year later, she moved out since her father got transferred. Either he had become too big for our small town or some place bigger than Shimoga required his bigness. Quite a few influential politicians of Karnataka are from Shimoga district though not one is as innocent or enchanting as the town itself. If you have an interest in history, you ought to know that Shimoga was the southern tip of Ashoka's Mauryan Empire. I am not sure if he ever visited Shimoga because this was in the 3rd B.C. At the same time, I really doubt if Emperor Ashoka would have missed out on the opportunity. For those of you interested in cinema, Malgudi Days was shot close to the town.

At one end of Shimoga was the bus stand. This was dusty and dirty and noisy. At another end was the railway station. This became dirty and noisy three times a day when the trains arrived and departed. The rest of the time, calm prevailed. Beyond the railway tracks, Shimoga tapered off into fields, wilderness and a hill, Ragi Gudda. Two minutes from the station was our house. A large part of my childhood was spent here.

What follows is a series of real-life tales, adventures and madness that took place a long time ago.

. . . .

(PART 1)

HALF PANT TALES FROM SHIMOGA

(1)

5 PAISE CHAPATI

It started out a Saturday like any other. I was in the fourth standard. It was the third and final period and Emilia Miss was teaching us science. Our attention drifted between the clock and the lesson. At the stroke of one, the weekend would begin and each of us had many plans. As we hoisted our heavy school bags and stepped out of the gate, Prashant and Yaseen walked up to me. Prashant's family owned a textile store that sold Raymond garments. Yaseen's family owned an ice factory. On most days, they had more pocket money than the rest of us and in the tradition of wealthy philanthropists, distributed alms to the needy regularly during recess. They didn't dole out money but bought us delectables in the form of *nalli kayi* (gooseberries), tender mango slices with salt and chilli powder, ice candies, *ajji koodlu* (literally meaning grandmother's hair; white in colour and a small-town version of cotton candy) etc.

Today however, they both handed me money, a 5 paise coin each along with big looks of gratitude. In return, I gave them the confident smile of a driving license agent assuring his customers that the job is as good as done. Prashant and Yaseen had only one thing on their minds: magnet. I am not sure how it started but one fine day, the story of an amazing discovery began doing the rounds *i.e.* if we placed a coin on the railway track and a train ran over it, the coin would turn into a magnet. All of us believed it

7

without a paisa of doubt. Since dad was a railway guard, I had unconditional access to the railway property and premises, unlike the general public. In that sense, I was part of a privileged lot.

I got home, gobbled up lunch quickly and ran across to Giddi's house, my friend in the railway quarters. Strangely, Giddi hadn't heard about this marvellous discovery but being the son of a railway guard himself, he didn't doubt it one paisa. In fact, he smiled as if he had known this truth in the womb. We hung around for a while sitting on a branch of the guava tree in his backyard. Many Saturday afternoons were spent here discussing life and various schemes. At 3:40 pm, we climbed down and ambled across to the platform. The Birur Mail was due at 4:15 pm. It usually had a few people alighting before the train headed to Talguppa after ten minutes. Generally, the station used to be quite deserted and we could carry out our sure shot experiment without much ado.

We walked to the end of the platform close to the loco shed where the tracks were at ground level. We carefully placed the two coins, one on each track and walked back onto the platform. Minutes later, the train chugged in and a few townspeople got off. We were at the edge of the platform and the engine halted right before us. We waved to the driver Andanappa uncle who smiled back. We saw the guard Sabapathy uncle at the far end signing some papers. A few minutes later, he waved the green flag. Giddi and I smiled at each other in anticipation. The engine wheezed to life blowing out the smoke of a thousand cigars and the train creaked into motion. Like a sumo wrestler pushed into a sprint, it lumbered slowly out of the platform gathering momentum. After seeing the LV board (LV stands for Last Vehicle and the final bogie of every train has to carry it), Giddi and I ran across to our spot. The coins weren't on the tracks where we had placed them. We bent down, sat on our haunches and started hobbling along the track. And then, a good 12 feet away, we found what had minutes earlier been purchasing power. Now they were metal amoebae. The coins were about four times their original size and had been pressed into shapes that I still can't describe.

It was the moment of truth. We had two magnets and an endless block of iron to attach them to. Excitedly, we put the coins on the track expecting them to stick but no such thing happened. Giddi and I looked at each other, confused. We tried again. Same result. Still on our haunches, we hobbled along placing the coins at different intervals. The coins refused to stick. Someone, somewhere had started a silly rumour that all of us had believed. And as easily as we had believed it, we now as easily dismissed it; after all, we had the lab reports in our hands.

Giddi: *Ella bhukali. Coinu magnet heng aagathe?*

(All of this is a big hoax. How can a coin become a magnet?)

Bhukali was our slang for a fib; an ingenuous lie.

I echoed Giddi's sentiment with as much aplomb.

Me: *Correctu. Magnettu ishtu simple-a? Haagidhre railway quarters alli ella sakkath dhuddu maadkond irauvru.*

(Right. Is making a magnet this simple? Then everyone in the railway quarters would have minted lots of money.)

I pocketed the two transformed but unsuccessful coins and we walked back home. They were now mementoes like the lunar rock the first visitors to the moon carried back with them. They didn't offer us a new or altered reality but were still priceless.

On Monday morning, Prashant, Yaseen and I reached school fifteen minutes before assembly, something that hadn't happened since LKG. They were as bouncy as sponge balls. Strangely, the weight of their expectations didn't affect me. I had had a day and a half to dismiss the farce in my head. I fished out the two metal amoebae from my pocket and before they could exult, told them with casual authority,

Me: *Yaavno sakkath bhukali hod dhidh aane. Magnettu illa, yenu illa!*

(Someone's fibbed big time. No magnet, nothing at all!)

Strangely, Prashant and Yaseen despite their weeklong anticipation and excitement expressed no huge disappointment. Such are the convictions of childhood; in some cases, one is so steadfast and in others, so fickle. They accepted the reality with the maturity of a lama. More wondrously, they were delighted.

The old story was forgotten at once as they marvelled at the coins. No one had seen coins as deformed and fanciful as the ones they now held. Tittering, Prashant exclaimed,
Prashant: *Bombaat! Aidh paise chapati! Kharaab aagidhe! Thanks Dabba.*
(This is fabulous! 5 paise chapati! Made very badly! Thanks Dabba.)
Bombaat was our slang for fabulous. *Dabba* was my nickname.

Prashant and Yaseen were wealthy but weren't particularly conversational or charming. Therefore, their interaction with the girls was much lower than what they hoped for, but not on this day. Through every class, the 5 paise chapatis sneaked their way into the hands of the students. The boys went wild, the girls nursed and coddled them with their fingers and Class IV B collectively owned a piece of mesmerising weirdness. The fame of the 5 paise chapatis spread to the rest of the school; the juniors came pleading, the seniors came demanding to see them. Prashant and Yaseen displayed what could have well been the Dead Sea Scrolls. The girls kept smiling at them while the seniors pooh-poohed them with envy. For a short, glorious time, the 5 paise chapatis propelled them to the top of the pack.

. . . .

(2)

MOLASSES

I was all of five years old. Dad was still a goods train guard and hadn't moved up to passenger trains. I was deeply fascinated by the goods trains and often pestered dad to take me with him to work. One Saturday, he finally told me that I could go along with him the next morning. Since it would be a Sunday, he could indulge me and I wouldn't miss out on my homework. I was so thrilled that I flitted all over the house.

Mom: *Anand, bugri tarah aadodh bekilla. Sumne koothko.*

(No need to spin around like a top. Sit still.)

Dad had consented because it was the shortest trip in his duty-sheet. The goods train with 26 wagons would leave Shimoga at eight in the morning. The destination was Bhadravati, barely 16 kilometres and 25 minutes away. Every few months, the train went to the sugar factory to bring back molasses. Laying out my clothes, mom told me explicitly to be careful.

Mom: *Shirt mele molasses bidhre, kare hogalla!*

(If you get molasses on your shirt, you can't get rid of the stain!)

After an early breakfast, she dressed me up, parted my hair neatly, tucked my shirt into my stretchlon shorts, reminded me again to stay away from the molasses and sent me off with dad. I was so happy that I walked two steps ahead and led him into the station. The driver Peer Saab and the fireman joined us. I asked dad if I could ride with them in the engine. Before he could say anything, the fireman lifted me up and said that I would drive the train. I lost my breath for a few seconds. I had wanted to do that all my life. The next day, the entire class would go crazy when they heard, for sure.

The engine was a monster. It always looked angry. Compared to that, dad's guard compartment was quite ordinary. It was a boring square box with nothing much inside. If these two ever got into a fight, the engine could kill dad's compartment with just its breath. So maybe to protect it, they always put the guard's compartment at the other end. I was a little disappointed that dad had decided to become a guard and not a driver. We headed in opposite directions of the train and when we reached the engine, the driver leapt into it easily. The fireman held me up and Peer Saab took me inside. As I stared at this metal monster and tried to make sense of it, the fireman opened the boiler. I had never seen so much fire in one place. He picked up a big shovel and fed it 25 times with coal. Noticing my amazed expression, he chuckled and remarked,

Fireman: *Haaktha idhre thinthane irathe.*

(If you keep on feeding, it will go on eating.)

I laughed. The driver was standing at the edge of the engine and looking at dad who must have been half a kilometre away at the other end. As soon as dad waved the flag, the driver lifted a heavy iron rod and let it down. The engine snorted, made a hefty noise and started moving. I clapped. As we reached the end of the platform, the fireman had stopped feeding the fire. He lifted me up and asked me to tug a long metal wire above. I pulled and the engine let out a shrill whistle. I had always imagined that there would be a button for this. Within a few minutes, we were on the bridge across the Tunga river. The river was famous for its sweet water and there was a saying: *Ganga snana, Tunga paana (Bathe in the Ganga and drink from the Tunga).* As we passed the huge girders of the bridge, they created a strange, vibrating sound. To me, this part was always scary yet exciting. Before long, we were passing through open fields. The driver and the fireman now had no work. I asked the driver if he could hold me outside the engine. I wanted to wave at dad. He shook his head. I begged him. He stood at the edge, peered down the train and said that dad wasn't standing outside. I asked him if I could also take a look. He held me tightly and tilted me out of the engine. He was right.

As we reached the outskirts of Bhadravati, the main tracks went straight and another set turned right. I didn't notice the driver do anything but the train turned right. I told myself that on the next trip, I would learn how to do this. The tracks led to the big gate of the sugar factory. We went inside and stopped the train. I helped by lifting the big, iron rod. The fireman jumped out with me in his arms. Soon, the four of us were together on the platform. Three people from the sugar factory joined us. I kept looking up, watching them talk. One of the factory employees said that they would start filling the wagons with two pipes and be done by late afternoon.

The four of us walked to the Running Room. This always made me laugh. How could a room that stood in one place be called a Running Room? I knew a lot about the railways but some things were beyond me. For instance, every station had a railway code: YPR for Yeshwanthpur, MYS for Mysore, TLG for Talguppa, ARS for Arasikere etc. For Shimoga, it was SMET. I always read SMET as Something. SHMG would have been better. The Running Room had three metal cots and I settled down next to dad. The driver and the fireman immediately took off their shirts. Both of them had big stomachs but the driver was clearly the winner. I noticed that their banians were very different. Dad always wore a half-sleeved white banian whereas they sported sleeveless, netted ones. One was red and the other was a pale yellow. So it wasn't just the shirt and the trousers but even the banian was a carefully considered part of the uniform. The drivers and the firemen wore dark blue clothes with coloured banians. The guards were given white because they travelled in a cleaner compartment. The Britishers had clearly thought of everything except maybe SMET.

Dad told me that we had nothing to do till four. He had also undressed and was in his banian and *punche* (a white cotton cloth), one that every respectable brahmin wrapped around his waist. They would now sleep for a few hours till lunch. Dad instructed me to rest as well. I nodded but deep down wondered what I had to rest from. We had travelled for about thirty minutes and the day had just begun. There was so much more to be done; 26 wagons had to be filled with molasses. The three of them lay down and soon enough began to snore. Mom always made fun of dad's snoring and on some mornings, she would look sleepy and irritated. Thank God she wasn't married to the driver or the fireman! She would have looked grumpy all her life. They made as much noise as the engine. There had to be some connection, I thought. Maybe they took in so much noise while driving that they had to let it out.

Suddenly, the silence around the snores felt very noticeable. The familiar sounds of a railway station were missing: the sounds of people walking and talking, of bogies being shunted in the background, an engine hissing or whistling, heavy pushcarts with crates being pulled on the platform etc. Instead, there was only the chirping of birds from a few directions. It was as if we had taken the train to the middle of nowhere, parked it and gone to sleep. I stepped out of the Running Room and gently closed the door behind me. On the platform it was just the goods train and me. Even the three factory-people had vanished inside. The train stood there looking neglected. It reminded me of J C Kiran who was in my class. He was quite a handful and would regularly invent mischief. In return, he was often made to kneel down in a corner of the classroom. No one was supposed to speak to him or acknowledge his presence. 'This gives me time and mind space to think of the next scheme.', he had smiled and confided in me once.

The wagons were all tankers. Each tanker had an opening on top, big enough for dad or me to get in. Two huge pipes had climbed the sides of the first two tankers. They looked like monster snakes. The other ends of the pipes were obviously inside the sugar factory. I wanted to go in and take a look but wasn't sure if I would be allowed. Molasses was being filled. I stood for a few minutes staring at the tankers and pipes. No one was there to check when the tankers would get filled and start overflowing. I felt someone was not doing his duty. Since I wasn't sleepy and this looked exciting, I decided to stand guard. But not being able to see the molasses and only imagining it going into the tankers was boring. So, I started walking and inspecting all the tankers. I found a long stick and made my way down the train, tapping each tanker. They all sounded the same. I was also tapping the joints connecting the tankers to make sure they were locked properly, else it could turn out to be disastrous. I reached dad's end of the train and everything looked fine.

On my way back, I spotted two kids at the head of the train. They looked about my age from where I stood, and were looking up at the tankers being filled. One of them touched the tanker, the other bent down and picked something off the ground and looked up again. I knew at once that they were molasses thieves. They were trying to work out a way to get to the molasses. I yelled and started running towards them. They saw me from a distance but held their ground. My first instinct was to prevent the crime. This was always better than trying to sort out the headaches once the theft happened. I reached the spot and was more than convinced about who they were and their intentions. They were in dirty and ill-fitting clothes, and one of them had stuff coming down his nose. It was gooey just like molasses but a pale yellow. I asked them gruffly,

Me: *Yen beko? Ee trainoo num tandhedu. Ille idhaare.*

(What do you want? This train belongs to my dad. He's right here.)

They stared at me.

Me: *Ondhu drop molasses kadhru jail-ge haak bidthaare.*

(If you steal even a drop of molasses, he'll put you in jail.)

They continued looking at me without saying anything. Clearly, they were buying time trying to think of a quick, safe reply. Before

they could come up with anything, I wanted the matter closed.
Me: *Helidhu artha aaglilva? Ee factory, trainoo...ella namdhe. Hogi!*
(Didn't you get what I said? This factory, train...everything is ours.
Leave!)
They didn't say a word, continued staring at me and walked off
slowly. They kept turning and looking at me. I kept my eyes on
them till they disappeared out of the gate. I didn't feel like a hero;
I was just doing my duty.

By now I was feeling hot and went back to the Running Room.
The big, white ceiling fans created air and noise in equal amounts.
I lay down next to dad. He stirred for a moment, opened his eyes
and closed them again. The next thing I remember was dad
waking me up. I had passed out for a few hours. It was already
lunchtime and they had dragged the wooden table to a spot
between the two cots. The driver and the fireman sat on one, dad
and I on the other. Their tiffin carriers were out. Between the two
of them, they had an enormous amount of rice. Two
compartments had gravy with chicken pieces in them. As they
wriggled themselves into comfortable positions,
Dad: *Neevu maadbidi. Naavu aamele maadtheevi.*
(You finish. We'll eat later.)
Driver: *Time aaythu saaar. Ellaru votge maadbidona.*
(It's time, Sir. Let's all eat together.)
Dad told them that there wasn't enough room at the table and that
we would start once they finished. He took me outside. I knew the
real reason: chicken. We were brahmins and didn't allow
ourselves to eat in the same room as non-vegetarians. We hung
around outside and I told dad about the molasses thieves. He said
that I shouldn't have interfered, that there were guards (security
and not railway) and no one could steal the molasses. Twenty
minutes later, the driver and the fireman stepped out, belching.
Everything that came out of them was loud. Dad and I went back
inside. They had cleared the table, washed their tiffin carriers and
put them back in the corner. Dad was still a little uneasy. He
pulled out the Deccan Herald, spread it on the table and opened

our lunch. There was sambar rice, pre-mixed curd rice and cabbage *palya* (sabzi). We ate in silence as we were both hungry. When we stepped out, I noticed two bidi stubs a few feet outside the door. One of the sugar factory personnel was chatting with the driver. The pipes had moved many tankers to the left and within fifteen minutes, the last two were being filled. As we washed our faces, dad pulled out his white handkerchief to wipe my face while the driver and the fireman pulled out coloured, checkered hankies. This uniform thing was so thoroughly thought out. I told myself that some day when I write a book, I will make special mention of this.

The journey back was uneventful. I again travelled with the driver but wasn't as excited as a first-timer. I did help with starting the engine and pulled the whistle a few times. But my mind was on the reaction in class the next morning. I kept wondering about the right thing to say: I rode the train or I drove the train? After a point, it became very confusing and I just enjoyed the breeze. By 4.45 pm, we were back in Shimoga. The platform was deserted. Dad and I got off. I told him that we should wait for the driver and the fireman, but he said that they had to shunt the wagons two tracks away and would take time. We reached home and mom gave dad filter coffee while I had Nutramul. Despite it being a Sunday, I didn't go out to play. Instead, I spent the next three hours telling mom every detail of the trip. She continued with her chores, listening and nodding. She didn't seem particularly curious; she only checked the back of my shirt for molasses stains.

· · · · · · · · · · · · · · · · · ·

(3)

MOSQUITO KUNG FU

It was the late 1970s and television was a good five years away. I was well into my sixth year of life and my brother Sriram was ahead by three years. School life was easy, play life was fun and evening life was routine, without much variety. We had to be back home from playing by 7:00 pm. Ten minutes of grace period was a grudging clause that was included. The next hour-and-a-half was for homework, followed by dinner. We could then sit around doing what we liked, till lights were switched off around 10 pm.

Dad occasionally got a Kannada magazine, Sudha or Taranga, from the lending library. Sometimes, he brought a copy of Competition Success Review. He would read out a small article to us and then play quizmaster with the General Knowledge quiz. This would take all of thirty minutes. Mom usually sat knitting sweaters, peeling peas or doing some time-consuming chore. After dad finished what I think he considered his fatherly duty, he would pick up the day's Deccan Herald despite having read every line earlier in the day. Sriram usually sat around with a faraway look, probably thinking of the Milky Way. We were very different, to say the least. I was mostly concerned with the 'here and now' while he usually carried the mien of a metaphysicist. It was then that I would get down to my mission.

Like nearly everyone else, I detest mosquitoes. Usually after the first showers, the railway quarters got infested with them. Every house had mosquito nets that came out at bedtime, but this was cure, not prevention. Despite shutting the windows a little before sunset, large armies of suckers would somehow get in. Every time I looked around the room, I would spot some on the walls and curtains, on the ceiling, a few buzzing around heads and a couple circling our feet, trying to land. Then there were those hiding behind the shoe racks, the sides of cupboards, the undersides of tables and other dark places. The buzzing, irritating horde of them drove me crazy. Still, it would seem that there weren't more than a dozen or so mosquitoes in each room. This was an understandable average for a house in a mosquito-infested area. But every time I would start killing and counting them, I would be stunned. I would end up with no less than about 180 mosquitoes. It was as if they had set up a production line somewhere in the house and even as I caught them, more would rush in to take their place. Agreed, after a point the numbers would start diminishing. But just when I would think to myself that I had seen the last of them, two more stragglers would come by, and then another two. My record (or maybe theirs) stands at a staggering 276 mosquitoes vanquished in a single evening. I would spend an hour every evening, hunting them down. Circling, I would cover the living room, the bedroom, our little dining room over and over. Dad always told me that I could never wipe out all of them and it was therefore a futile pursuit. I always responded that just because *asuras* cropped up endlessly, could the Gods resign and give up battling them? I used to hunt them down, not kill them. Over months of total focus and practice, I had reached an unheard-of level of dexterity:

Level 1 – With my forefinger, I would tap a mosquito with just that amount of pressure so that it fell down unconscious. (It didn't matter if the mosquito was on the wall, on a drape or on my brother's foot.)

Level 2 – If the mosquito was flying around, I grabbed it in my fist and held it for just that period of time till it became unconscious. (I can recollect only a few times when I opened my fist and the mosquito either flew away or was squished.)

Level 3 – I caught the fat ones that were already a little drunk and lethargic, between my thumb and forefinger. It made no difference whether they were on the wall or flying around mid-air like a Zeppelin. Again, the squeeze carried just that amount of pressure to make them unconscious but not kill.

I could do all three of the above with either hand. I had become a Shaolin. But what gave me immense joy was what came afterward. Each comatose mosquito went into a little rectangular plastic box, one slightly bigger than a matchbox. At 10 pm, I would retire with this box next to my ear. The mosquitoes would slowly regain consciousness and start buzzing in their efforts to escape. Imagine the collective, desperate sound of two hundred odd mosquitoes! I know it sounds morbid but this had become my lullaby. It was my revenge for the bites and harassment of the past few hours. Over fifteen minutes, the drone would gradually peter out and I would whisper to the box through clenched teeth,

Sleepy Me: *Mosquitoes are now mosquietoes!*

The next morning, I would tear a fresh sheet of white paper from my notebook and put all the carcasses on it. I would place this scrunched piece of paper on a slab behind the house, come down on it with a stone, see the splatter of my family's blood and let out a victorious Shaolin shriek.

. . . . ● ● ● ● ● ● ● ● ● . . . . . .

(4)

ALLAH'S SCHOOL BAG

I was in upper kindergarten at Mary Immaculate, the school quite a few of us from the neighbourhood attended. The school was a couple of kilometres away and we travelled back and forth in a *kudre gaadi* (horse cart). One tonga could carry about twelve of us, and our area had been divvied up between Kalandhar and Ghouse.

Kalandhar was an old man and his horse Mumtaz was equally frail. Ghouse's horse Jaanu was younger and much faster, just like him. Sadly, I was in Kalandhar's tonga. Ghouse's tonga would whistle past ours and that gang always won the race to school and back. They teased us often saying that we travelled in a bullock cart. I told mom on several occasions that I wanted to switch but Ghouse's tonga had no vacancy. Mom always responded that what mattered more was the school I went to and not the tonga I travelled in. She could never understand the bigness of small things. Each day, we would urge Kalandhar to go faster. He never yielded and always said the same thing,

Kalandhar: *Mumtaz kaalige nau od banbid thathe!*

(Pain will come running to Mumtaz's legs!)

His reaction was horse-laugh-funny to all of us. We would giggle but curse him inwardly for what he put us through. On the underside of the tonga was a big gunny cloth, doubled up and nailed at the four corners. All the school bags went into it.

21

Because of the weight, the cloth sagged and held the bags safely.

One day, we finished school as usual and headed home. Three of us from my street were the last ones to get off the tonga. One friend stayed next door and the other, five houses away in the opposite row. When I jumped off and bent down to take my bag, I froze. My academic life was missing. For a moment, I wondered if I had left it behind in class but then clearly remembered putting the bag into the tonga. Mom came out and I nervously told her that my bag must have fallen off somewhere along the way. She made the same face that she made whenever I refused to eat bitter gourd. I told Kalandhar to turn the tonga around. He was slow and reticent as usual.

Kalandhar: *Namduge namaazige hog beku.*

(I have to go for my namaaz.)

Mom told him sternly that we had to look for the bag first. Though a Kannadiga, she had grown up in Delhi and had consequently spent years living closer to Indira Gandhi compared to the rest of us. That had to count for something. Muttering under his breath, Kalandhar said `*Hui!*' and his old horse moved. I told him that I didn't care about the pain in the horse's leg and that he should charge forward with speed. Kalandhar took out the whip and whacked Mumtaz. He was hoping that she still had some youth hidden somewhere in her body. Mumtaz neighed saying she will do her best. And the best she managed was Mohinder Amarnath's run up.

We were soon out of Basavanagudi, crossed Nehru Stadium and kept trotting towards the school. I kept peering towards the other side of the road. The traffic was quite heavy and so was the honking, primarily due to a handsome number of emaciated cows along the way. Kalandhar kept saying that it was foolish to expect my bag to be found, as either some kid would have picked it up or a bus would have run over it. I asked him to pray that somehow, I find it. I added that I didn't mind losing the bag. Mom would buy me a new one and then remind me often to be extra careful. But I had to get my books back. They contained all my notes and homework. Like a cow, Kalandhar shook his head slowly. Everything in his life, starting with his own, was hopeless. Kalandhar: *Kitaboon hasu thin bidthathe. Kitaboon gaayab aag bidthathe.* (The cows will eat the books. The books will vanish.)

His sentence was pathetic, but his thinking was probably right. Almost every day, we witnessed cows eating paper. My bag contained good quality Lekhak notebooks and I was sure it was a sought-after flavour. As we reached the school gates, my optimism had grown as flimsy as my stretchlon shorts. We stopped for a minute to let Mumtaz gather herself. While she made incoherent noises, (*throoofffphhuuuu* being the most recognizable), I filled myself with pseudo-hope and ordered Kalandhar to turn the tonga around.

We were obviously on the left of the road, and this was the right side, since my bag had fallen off on the way home. We headed back slowly through the thick evening traffic of inter-city buses, inter-area autos, intermittent scooters, interminable cyclists and intolerable, purposeless cows. I was straining forward on my seat, eyeing the street. Suddenly, I yelled so loudly that Mumtaz froze in fright. I had spotted the red corner of my bag. Miraculously, it was lying on the side of the road in front of DVS Senior College, covered in dirt. I jumped off the tonga, picked it up and smiled displaying teeth bigger than Mumtaz's. Everything was intact. I wiped the mud off the bag, kissed it and jumped back onto the tonga. As we rode home, Kalandhar went on about how he'd been so sure that we would never find it. For the remainder of our journey, he kept shaking his head and repeating his belief. When we reached home, I jumped off the tonga, kissed Mumtaz on her side and sprinted inside.

Kalandhar: *Allah-ge nimduge baala ishta.*

(Allah likes you very much.)

After that day, Kalandhar always kept my bag next to him. It never went tumbling into the gunny cloth with the rest of the school bags.

. . . .

(5)

THE SEA BENEATH MY HOUSE

It was born in 1975. By the time it swam all the way from America to Shimoga, it was 1978. The first bunch of classmates who watched Jaws said that it was *bombaat* (fantastic). Avinash, among the strongest and most fearless in our class, told me that there was Jaws in Koodli, a place twelve kilometres from Shimoga. Here, our Tunga river met the Bhadra river and became Tungabhadra. He remarked that Jaws needed a lot of water and if we were lucky, we could spot it at Koodli. But first, I had to see the movie.

On a Sunday afternoon, I accompanied Sumanth, Amogha and his mom as we walked to HPC Talkies, barely a kilometre from home. Sumanth had aunts and cousins in America and his parents frequently travelled there. Amogha's dad was a college lecturer and his mom looked and came across as one, though she was a housewife. Their families were clearly more progressive and exposed to influences compared to mine. Thankfully for me, Sumanth and Amogha were close friends and stayed near my house, just beyond the railway quarters.

We entered the packed hall with great anticipation. After a few Kannada movie trailers, whistles turned to whispers. There was a palpable silence of trepidation. As the first scene of the movie unfolded, we squealed, `*Jaws will come! Jaws will come!*' Minutes passed and there was no sign of Jaws. We kept urging the boat to go deeper into the ocean. An irritated man in the front row asked us to shut up. When Jaws finally appeared, I stopped breathing. It was the most terrifying scene I'd ever seen. The entire ocean was inside my mind. I felt that I would splutter and drown. My nails were deep into Sumanth's arm, deeper than what Jaws could have probably managed with its teeth. With each passing minute, the drama turned into trauma. I wasn't even sure if I was looking forward to what came next. I grew furious with the people in the movie for having gone into the ocean in the first place. I thought of our adventurous Kannada movies and they made me look forward to every scene. Dr. Rajkumar, Vishnuvardhan, Ambarish etc. also performed heroic deeds but on land where they had much more control. In our films, if the hero knew that Jaws was lurking somewhere, he would never venture out in a boat and then shudder and suffer. When the ordeal finally ended, my lungs didn't have the strength to even heave a sigh of relief. I walked out looking like a two-day-old idli. Sumanth and Amogha seemed fine while Amogha's mom looked all-appreciative, which I couldn't fathom.

On our walk back, the three of them discussed scenes and chatted animatedly. Every time they looked towards me for my contribution, I made big eyes and said `*Aiyo!*' which I hoped made them feel that the movie had left me mightily impressed. Like in other languages, Kannada is also blessed with a versatile word that stands for many things depending on how one utters it. `*Aiyo!*' can communicate nonchalance, compassion, awe and more. I reached home and told mom that Jaws was magical and that she had to watch it. She had been difficult with me that morning and I wanted her to suffer equally.

Mom: *Adheno dhoddu meen anthe! Thoo!*

(I believe it's about a big fish. Rubbish!)

Even as a concept, anything non-vegetarian threw us off.

Me: *Meen all amma. JAWSU!*

(Not a fish, mom. JAWS!)

But she didn't seem interested and I let it go. The next morning, as usual I went in for my bath. Our backyard had been turned into a bathroom. Dad had divided the small backyard by building a seven-foot wall in the middle. The right side was open and had a few plants and two guava trees. The left side was covered with an asbestos sheet and this was our bathroom. The original railway quarter's bathroom was inside the house and we used it for washing clothes and utensils. With more ingenuity and less money, dad had created this additional space. In one corner of the bathroom, he had put up a coarse cement block with a big cavity, into which a sizeable brass boiler had been placed. Underneath the boiler was a small fireplace. Every morning, dad woke up at six, lit pieces of firewood and boiled water. He would get down on his knees, bend low and blow into the fireplace with a hollow iron rod. It looked like a flute except that it lacked the top-holes that would have made it more mellifluous. It made the fire crackle the wood. If dad was on train duty, mom did it. Once Sriram and I grew up, we took over this task. The bathroom also had a square, three feet deep cement tank that held cold water. I filled the bucket with eight mugs of boiling water. I then dipped the plastic mug into the cold-water tank. Because of the asbestos roof above, not much sunlight entered the bathroom and the water tank was the colour of cement. So even though it was only three feet deep, it looked much deeper and dark. I looked in and saw the sea underneath the water tank. It extended across the railway quarters and beyond the town. It reached up to Koodli and merged with the Jaws' sea. Jaws was lurking somewhere and the minute I would dip the plastic mug, it would shoot right up.

The previous night, I had slept peacefully and hadn't thought of Jaws at all. But now, out of the blue, my mind was filled with this mad creature. I kept telling myself that it was all *bhukali* (a wild, untrue imagination). But my hand stayed frozen over the tank, my mind gripped with fear. Minutes passed and the hot water was losing its warmth. Mom was in the kitchen making breakfast. She always heard the sound of water when I had my bath. She called out asking if everything was okay. I shouted back that I was fine. With the absolute tips of my thumb and forefinger, I held the edge of the mug handle. Shaking like a chandelier during an earthquake, I shut my eyes, dipped the mug into the water and scooped up a few drops. I did this around 30-40 times before I managed a mug of cold water into the bucket. Each time I dipped the tip of the mug, I was sure it would be the last thing I did. I finally had an insufficient bath with just nine mugs of lukewarm water. This continued the next day and for three weeks more. At some point, I gradually managed to calm my mind and started having regular baths. In the years ahead, I did learn to swim in the pumpset and the Tunga river. But every now and then, Mr. Spielberg's pet would pay me an unannounced visit.

. . . .

(6)

WHY? UNNECESSARY!

If you come today, it's too early
If you come tomorrow, it's too late
You pick the time
Tik tik tik tik tik tik, Tik tik tik tik tik tik
Tik tik tik tik tik tik, Tik tik tik tik tik tik
Daaarling!

The crowd was in raptures and the whistles wouldn't stop. I didn't know how to whistle and so made shrill noises. The singer sounded exactly like Dr. Rajkumar. The year was 1979. Over the past few months, this song had become one of the greatest anthems in the history of Kannada movies. It was also the only Kannada song with only English words. The movie Operation Diamond Rocket had come out at the end of 1978 and from the moment of its release, it had taken over everyone's life.

It was *Ganpati habba* (Ganesha festival) time and we were at the biggest pandal in the railway quarters. It was Orchestra Day, the most looked-forward-to-evening across nine days of cultural events. Sampath Orchestra Company was only on its sixth song of the evening and had already created a storm. While I took in the music, I'd grown transfixed by the drummer. He was at the ack, not as well-lit as the others and regularly got blocked from my view by the singer. He didn't get as much attention as the rest of the troupe but in my eyes, he was something else. Every time he did *tigi-digi-tugu-dugu-dugu -dugu-dugu-dugu-dishhh!*, I would jump involuntarily from where I was sitting on the ground, my bottom rising right off. I had no control over it. That evening, I must have done this over a hundred times. When the second verse had started, I was spellbound.

Million drums beat in my heart
Million dreams haunt my heart
Million desires spring in my heart
Million memories seize my heart

Whoever had written this song, had written this stanza with me in mind. Nothing had ever excited me more than the sound of drums. I couldn't take my eyes off the drummer the entire evening. After an hour, they took a 15-minute break. During this time, a young guy performed breakdance. He did the *bus, glass wall* and *bottle*. It was magical. By the end of his performance, I had decided that I wanted to be a drummer by profession and a breakdancer in my spare time. The orchestra ended at 11:30 pm but I couldn't sleep till four in the morning.

The next day, I spoke to a few boys from the pandal about the Sampath Orchestra Company. I didn't get clear answers but they said that some of the older people could help me get in touch with them. That evening, after finishing my homework, I decided to inform dad and ask his permission. Mom was in the kitchen giving the final touches to dinner while he was reading the Deccan Herald.

Me: *Appa, nimige yeno helbeku.*

(Dad, need to tell you something.)

I told him that I loved the orchestra and desperately wanted to join Sampath. Dad lowered the newspaper and looked at me in confusion.

Dad: *Orchestra na?*

(Orchestra?)

Me: *Haudh appa. Thumba talent beku but ee vaisalle shuru maadhre mundhe yen aaro aag bahudu.*

(Yes dad. It requires a lot of talent but if I start early, I might become someone in the future.)

Dad looked a little heavy on his face.

Dad: *Ananda, Michael Jackson aagthya?*

(Will you become Michael Jackson?)

I said, `No!'. I emphatically told him I didn't want to be Michael Jackson. I wanted to be a drummer and for that, I had to join an orchestra.

Dad: *Michael Jacksonu, drumsu, orchestra, tabla…ella ondhe.*

(Michael Jackson, drums, orchestra, tabla…it's all the same.)

If I were a couple of years younger, I would have lost it with dad. Thankfully, I was seven and had the maturity to deal with his narrow mindedness. I told him that each thing that he had mentioned was different, and that I had specifically spoken about drumming. Dad patiently heard me out but every word I spoke added more heaviness on his face.

Dad: *Yakappa? Beda! Chennagi odhi mundh barbeku, ashte!*

(Why? Unnecessary! Study well and get ahead, that's all!)

He said that and went back to the newspaper. His tone left the conversation open to further discussion but his turning away signalled that this was his final word on the subject. I stopped short, continued the argument in my head and won it. But it was a theoretical victory. I was grumpy during dinner and for the next week but slowly made my peace with it. I never again brought it up because I didn't want to upset him. But my love for drums continued. Every *Ganpati habba*, I went behind the pandal, tried to get as close to the band and never took my eyes off the drummer.

Four months went by and the world's greatest movie came to Shimoga: 36 Chambers of Shaolin. On a Sunday afternoon, I went to Mallikarjuna Talkies with Amogha and Sumanth and came out profoundly changed. I wanted to play drums and learn kung fu. Beyond this, if I had spare time, I would learn breakdance. I came home and practised the moves, not just that day but for weeks after. Two months later, 10 Brothers of Shaolin released. This added more variety to my moves. After this, there was no respite. Mallikarjuna Talkies was screening kung fu movies every month. Snake in the Monkey's Shadow released a month later, followed by The Drunken Monk, The Fearless Hyena, Drunken Master and Snake in the Eagle's Shadow. It was as if someone had mistakenly left a bag containing all these movies on the banks of the Tunga river, and the owner of Mallikarjuna Talkies had accidently found it while taking a dip.

To harden my knuckles, I started hitting walls, the Godrej almirah, tree trunks and anything else I came across. Mom would be in the kitchen and suddenly hear a dhunk.

Mom: *Anand, yeno adhu soundu?*

(What is that sound?)

This became her common refrain. I started a new regimen. I piled up sand on the terrace and in the afternoons, it got hot in no time. On Sundays, I started doing knuckle push-ups on sand. Our small backyard held two large guava trees (one bore white guavas and the other red) and a small banana plant. When no one was around, I would punch the tree trunks. I never tried that with the banana plant as I could have killed it with just one punch. When I went for my bath, I would fill two buckets with water and try lifting them. My aim was to hold them till a count of ten. My obsession took over my inability and helped me up to a count of three, occasionally even four and a few seconds more. The mark of an accomplished Shaolin monk was the nine dots on his pate and that was one of my big desires. Shaving my head was unthinkable. We only did that when one's parent passed away. So, on a Sunday, when everyone had stepped out, I called Giddi over. I took out white Camlin poster paint and asked him to apply the dots on my hair. He found it amusing as well as inspiring and carried out the task with the focus of a serious disciple. I tilted my head down in order to see the dots in the mirror. Since Giddi was a novice, I looked more foolish than accomplished. I quickly scrubbed soap on my hair and washed the paint off. The other desire was to have cloth shoes. We had a sewing machine at home. I was confident of stitching them but in the end, it turned out to be very complex and I gave up.

And then Fist of Fury released. We didn't know if Bruce Lee was a real person or a myth. It didn't matter. To us, he was God. His fighting style drove us wild. Shaolin style involved too much bending (bent fingers, bent knees, bent elbows, bent neck) and looked arduous and painful. Bruce Lee was lithe, his moves free flowing. He didn't indulge in any of the elaborate preparation that the Shaolin monks did before hitting. The Big Boss released and we said, `The Big Boss has arrived!'. I had never cared much about my looks but now I wanted small, slanted eyes. Obviously, even I knew that this was not to be. But karate was another way to be more like Lee! I discarded all my Shaolin moves and urged the rest of the gang to focus on karate. `Karate Chops' became my most commonly used phrase. If someone pulled my leg, did a misfield during cricket or said anything disagreeable, I always said,
Me: *Karate Chops kodla?*
(Shall I give you Karate Chops?)
We started training hard practising front, side and roundhouse kicks, as well as front flips. We would stand on the grass and without using our hands, bend down and flip forward with a certain amount of force. Initially, we landed on our backs. With weeks of practice, we had managed to land on our bums. The idea was to land on our feet so that we would be in a ready position to strike. We called these Dolphin Dives. The other move that we practised everyday was to lie down on our backs and using our hands and feet try and propel ourselves into a standing position. This was a must to become a karateka and sadly, I never managed this.

One day, I heard that karate classes were being held at the railway school. A private tutor had started teaching in the evenings, in one of the classrooms and anyone could join. I ran there after my school. Standing outside the window, I watched kids younger and older go through their exercises. I was overjoyed. This was five minutes from home and didn't cost much. I decided to learn my basics here and move to a bigger school in the future. Dad was back from his duty and reading the

Deccan Herald.

Me: *Appa, nimige yeno helbeku.*

(Dad, need to tell you something.)

He lowered the newspaper and looked at me in confusion. Maybe there was something in my tone that gave it away each time.

Me: *Appa, nanige karate kali beku.*

(Dad, I want to learn karate.)

He looked at me longer than usual, this time with more heaviness on his face. He finally sighed and with a plea in his voice,

Dad: *Yen rowdy aag beka?*

(Do you want to be a rowdy?)

I hadn't heard anything so bizarre and was stumped. I also got very emotional.

Me: *Baige bandiddu helthiddeera! Karate-gu rowdygu yen connection?*

(You are talking without thinking! What's the connection between karate and a rowdy?)

He remarked that he couldn't think of anyone other than rowdies who would be interested in karate. I remarked in my head that I couldn't think of anyone more idiotic than him.

Me: *Appa, Bruce Lee yen rowdy aagidna? Devru aagidda!*

(Dad, was Bruce Lee a rowdy? He was God!)

My words came out as swiftly as Bruce Lee's punches. Dad took a while to recover. Just like Bruce Lee, I was alert for any countermove. After a couple of minutes, he spoke in Shankaracharya's voice,

Dad: *Avna bidu. Avrella haavu thinkondu, karate kalth kondu hod dhaadthaare. Naavu brahmanru!*

(Forget him! All those people eat snakes, learn karate and keep fighting. We are brahmins!)

Honestly, I had no response to this. How can you respond to a brahmin who's been bitten by a mad snake? I told him firmly that he was wrong. He went back to his Deccan Herald. I was seething and wanted to let out a Bruce Lee wail of anger. I held myself back but decided not to give in this time. I just had to figure a smarter way to do this.

Meanwhile, I continued watching karate classes in the

evenings and practising on my own. A couple of months later, we were studying Gandhiji's 'My Confession' in class. It was a small chapter that dealt with Gandhiji writing a letter to his dad apologizing for having stolen money. The description of Gandhiji's father's nature seemed similar to dad's. During class, I decided that this was the best option. I wrote a letter to dad telling him how much I loved karate and how wrong he was about rowdies. Then, I added that in exchange for letting me learn karate, I would obey whatever he told me and never fight with Sriram. That night when his bed was ready, I slipped the letter under his pillow. He would surely discover it either before sleeping or after waking up. When I was having Nutramul the next morning, dad spoke to me in a very gentle voice.

Dad: *Anand, letter sikthu.*

(Got your letter.)

He smiled. It had moved him.

Dad: *Volledu! Chennagi bardidya but ondh vichara artha aaglilla.*

(Good! You've written it well but I didn't understand one thing.) I was ready to explain every letter of the letter. Dad asked that if he didn't allow me to learn karate, did it mean I wouldn't obey him and wouldn't stop fighting with Sriram? I was flummoxed. I mumbled that obviously, I hadn't meant that but he rejoined that my letter had given him this impression. From a very simple man, he had become wily. He added that obeying him, mom and Sriram could not have any pre-conditions. He then sighed and said,

Dad: *Yakappa? Beda! Chennagi odhi mundh barbeku, ashte!*

(Why? Unnecessary! Study well and get ahead, that's all!)

I had made two honest attempts and played by the book. It had got me nowhere. So, I decided that henceforth, I would play by my rules: behind the back. That very weekend, I made my own *nunchaku.* I went up the guava tree, cut two portions of a branch, shaved them with a knife to make them smooth and uniform. There was an old metal trunk at home that was hardly used. It was filled with stuff that would never be used but could never be thrown. On the inside, between the lid and the base at either end, was a small length of an iron chain. They served no purpose for the trunk. With great difficulty, I unhooked both chain lengths. With even more difficulty, I joined them together by opening one link and inserting the end of the other chain into it. Using regular nails, I drove the end links of the chain into the wooden rods. My handmade, homemade *nunchaku* was ready. I gingerly did my moves and it held itself together. With great difficulty and planning, I managed to hide it every day so that no one ever came across it. Whenever I had the house to myself, I practised. I did hit the back of my head quite frequently and it only made my resolve stronger. But I had too many demands on my time and there was the additional disadvantage of training alone. A few months into this, I slowly lost steam and sold it to another aspiring karateka in exchange for a brand new *bugri* (top) and ten marbles.

Over the next few years, I managed a handy and handsomely large list of all the things that invited dad's `Why? Unnecessary!' response. Like most brahmins, his mind was filled with an assortment of things that we weren't supposed to indulge in. Here is a fraction of the list:

1. Drums & most other instruments
2. Karate & breakdance
3. Trousers made of material other than cotton or terylene
4. Combing hair backwards
5. Anklet shoes & V-neck t-shirts
6. Longish sideburns
7. Sports cycle & sunglasses
8. Rolled-up shirtsleeves

. . . .

(7)

SECTION 302

It was a regular weekday morning, and I was in the midst of my routine. I was in the tiny meditation centre, devoid of any distraction. Here, my mind was always at its clearest and effortlessly locked into whatever I focused on. Today, I was reflecting upon the might and grandeur of the Chola dynasty. It was part of the curriculum and I had to memorize various names, dates and sequence of events. Sitting on my haunches in the toilet, I looked down and saw blood. I froze. Strangely I felt no pain. Confused and rattled, I cleaned up and stepped out. I briefly deliberated if mom needed to know this. Swinging towards safety, I hesitantly told her I was unwell. She felt my forehead and asked me how I was feeling. I blurted out the details and mentioned that I had no pain, thankfully. With her palm still on my forehead, she thought deeply. She then patted my cheek lightly and said,

Mom: *Aiyo! Yenu illa! Beetroot kano!*

(Oh! It's nothing at all! Beetroot!)

I turned red with anger and said that her choice of stupid vegetables was affecting me psychologically, as well as academically. Now, I had to redo my revision of the Chola dynasty from scratch. She nonchalantly went back to preparing breakfast.

The previous night, when we had sat down for dinner, I'd looked at my plate and groaned. It was one of 'those days' reserved for one of `those vegetables'. Mom was a good cook but every now and then (more often than this suggests), she marred her reputation by preparing awful vegetables. I liked potatoes, ladies finger, cucumber, peas, carrots, cauliflower, drumsticks and brinjal. So, we clearly had a choice of eight vegetables for seven days of the week. I never understood mom's compulsion to stray beyond these. On top of that, she had a ready benefit assigned to each of them. The beetroot sabzi on my plate looked like the scene of a ghastly crime. I told mom what I felt about it. She scolded me,

Mom: *Thin beku! Blood pressure-ge volledhu.*

(You have to have it! It's good for your blood pressure.)

I reminded her that she was serving me and not *thatha* (grandfather). I was eight years old and didn't have blood pressure. She retorted that if I ate it regularly, I wouldn't suffer from blood pressure when I reached *thatha's* age. I replied that I would start eating beetroot when I was sixty years old. I also told her that her logic was backfiring; the sight of beetroot was giving me blood pressure. She glared and started her meal. It was clear that I had no choice. Groaning, I somehow managed to finish it.

An incident like this occurred every week. Mom had too many friends and thereby, I had too many enemies: *Soorna Gadde* (Sooran), *Kumblu kayi* (Pumpkin), *Avre kayi* (Beans), *Tonde kayi* (Gherkin), *Chappradavre kayi* (Flat Beans), *Baale kayi* (Raw Banana), *Kosu* (Cabbage), *Navil Kosu* (Kohlrabi), *Donne mensin kayi* (Capsicum) and *Seeme badne kayi* (this is not even worthy of another name in any other language). To these ten, I will now add the dreadful Gourd Brothers: *Padawal kayi* (Snake Gourd), *Sore kayi* (Bottle Gourd), *Heere kayi* (Ridge Gourd), *Haagal kayi* (Bitter Gourd). Each one was more repulsive than the other; the Gourds were a totally cursed family.

A couple of weeks later, it was *dindu*, the inner part of the banana stem. The banana plant was sociable and useful on the outside but deep inside it was foul. As I moaned looking at my plate, mom scolded me yet again.

Mom: *Thin beku! Kalli ge volledhu.*

(You have to have it! It's good for stones.)

I told her that I wasn't a stone and deserved food worthy of a human. Either she missed the pun or ignored it. She asked me to shut up and said that *dindu* would dissolve the stones within my body. I knew that she meant well but the way she said things made me feel that my body was a playground for all ailments. Twenty-three minutes later, dindu was inside me working on my stones. We had a banana plant in our small backyard and I decided to test mom's theory. I picked up 4-5 tiny stones. Dad had a *dabna* (a big needle for sewing torn gunny bags) at home. Using that, I shoved the tiny stones into the thick stem. For my own sanity, I either had to prove her right or call her bluff. Three days later, I disfigured a part of the stem and probed inside. The stones stared back angrily for disturbing them. I called mom to the backyard and showed her the stones. She screamed at me for ruining the stem. I told her that she was actually angry because I had exposed her *bhukali* theories. Anyway, none of my attempts saved me from her readed vegetables. I continued to suffer and joke bleakly about them.

One day, I was reading an article in Deccan Herald about a murder. It said that the culprit had been booked under IPC Section 302 and would be imprisoned for life. I pulled a sheet out of my long notebook and made a big list of all the vegetables I hated. On top, I wrote IPC Section (with black sketch pen) and 302 (with red sketch pen) and pasted it on the kitchen wall. I told mom that all these were Section 302 vegetables and deserved to be imprisoned for life. She laughed, borrowed my sketch pen and put down days of the week next to each.

· · · · · · · · · · · · · · · · · · · ·

(8)

RED CARD

I looked carefully at the yellow card in my hand. The tally stood at one rupee seventy-five paise. For someone in the 2nd standard, it was a good effort. I had just started and knew that I would fare better. As I handed the card back to the shopkeeper, he turned his attention to the next customer. With all my strength, I fought the temptation to indulge myself with a peppermint. That would be a straight five paise off. I turned and briskly walked away from the shop.

It was a petty shop at the edge of the railway quarters, five minutes from home. I came here once or twice a week to buy peppermint or *paise-biscuits* or *boti*. *Paise-biscuits* were quite a thing, tiny in size but big on economy. They cost half a paisa per biscuit. Simple math but sometimes, the fundamentals must be stated: For five paise, one could get ten biscuits as against one peppermint. I loved peppermints but once in a while, quantity tempted me more. I would put five biscuits in each pocket and run away happily to play whatever game was being played. At regular intervals, I would alternate my consumption from each pocket. *Boti* had a different kind of allure. It was a long, yellow, hollow, cylindrical fried papad. Each *boti* was longer than my longest finger and cost five paise. The ritual of eating a *boti* was to stick it around a finger and slowly bite it off. If one had a *boti* around his finger while playing cricket or *gilli danda*, any misfield or slackness was usually forgiven. I must add that this behaviour of mixing food and play wasn't encouraged though. A big fantasy for most of us was to at some point, have ten *botis*, one on each finger.

Four months earlier, I was standing at this shop wondering whether to buy peppermints or *paise-biscuits*. While I was deciding, the shopkeeper turned to attend to another boy. He was about three years older than me and looked richer too. He was probably not from the railway quarters; most likely from the bordering area. He pulled out 25 paise from his pocket. Seeing so much money, I forgot my own purchase and was thinking what he would go for: 5 *botis*? One on each finger? That would be a sight! Or 50 *paise-biscuits*? Feeling embarrassed to pull out my five paise with him around, I waited for his transaction to finish. The shopkeeper turned around, and from behind a large aluminium box, took out a stack of cards held together with a rubber band. There were yellow, red and blue cards. He flipped through them and pulled out a blue one. It had various columns with the number 25 printed in them. Many 25s had been crossed with a pen. He took the 25 paise coin from the boy, crossed one more and put the card back into the stack. The boy walked away with a little dance in his walk.

Shopkeeper: *Yen beku?*

(What do you want?)

Right then, peppermints, *paise-biscuits* and *botis* were the most distant things in my mind.

Me: *Yen adhu?*

(What is that?)

Shopkeeper: *Savings Card.*

I asked him to tell me more. From the stack, he pulled out a fresh card. The card face was largely blank except for two printed lines, for the name and address of the customer. It also proudly carried his shop's name in capital letters: MANDANNA'S STORE. The reverse of the card looked mathematically scientific. Each card had five columns with ten rows, followed by a half-column of five rows. Every cell had numbers printed in them. Yellow had the number 5, red had 10 and blue, 25. This meant that the yellow one was a 5-paise card and so on. The first five columns of the yellow card added up to two rupees fifty paise. You could purchase a yellow card and every time you deposited 5 paise, Mandanna would cross one number on it. Once the card was complete, he gave you the entire amount. It was the money you had saved up, and you could do crazy things with it. But the card was only complete when the sixth half-column was also complete. That was his forcing-you-to-save fee. On a yellow card, one had to forego 25 paise, 50 on the red and one rupee twenty-five paise on the aristocratic blue. It was honestly fair. He had the cards printed, kept them carefully, made you save over months and was entitled to charge a small amount for it. I was spellbound. This was a very level-headed scheme. Sacrificing my weekly treats for months would turn out to be a hard bargain but the amount of money at the end of it would significantly alter my life. I couldn't think of a better savings plan for my pocket money.

Me: *Anand S, 116/A, Railway Quarters.*

I handed over the 5 paise coin as he wrote down my details. I was the proud holder of a yellow card. As I walked back, the dance in my steps was so much better than the boy's. I didn't want anyone to discover this beautiful secret and so kept mum about it. I trained myself off peppermints and other silly, fleeting temptations. I enjoyed them only when someone else bought them. To compensate for this, I started eating a lot more home goodies such as jaggery, groundnuts and copra. Every time I got a 5 paise coin, I ran to Mandanna's store. A few weeks went by and I had yet to complete a column. In my notebook, I had meticulously drawn a copy of the card. This exactly reflected Mandanna's tally. Apart from this, I had drawn three more cards, all fantasy versions. In these, I would cross out many columns, let my dreams race ahead of me and feel delighted. It had become an obsession but a good one.

A few weeks later, mom announced on a Sunday that she

wasn't making breakfast. *Sankranthi*, a big festival for us, was around the corner. She would get busy for a few days with the preparations. She enjoyed such occasions but usually got worked up too. Heading into a festival, she preferred a break from her usual chores so that she could focus on the big act. The standard practice was to get dosas from Gayathri Bhavan. She gave Sriram the money and asked him to fetch breakfast. Each plain dosa cost 25 paise and Sriram and I would have two each. Suddenly, my yellow card sprang to mind and became infinitely more important than breakfast. I knew I would suffer till lunch but to beget something, I had to reject something. My share of dosas cost fifty paise. In one visit, I would be able to cross out an entire column. I told mom that instead of Sriram getting dosas for both of us, I would rather take my fifty paise, go to the hotel and have them hot. Mom mumbled something about both being the same and that it was better if Sriram brought them home and that she didn't have fifty paise and that she needed change for five rupees and trailed off. With each `and' in her sentence, my yellow card drifted farther. I was forced into acting impetuously.

Me: *Amma! nanige dose beda! Aivathu paise beku!*

(Mom! I don't want dosas! I want 50 paise!)

I blurted this out more sharply than I had intended to and mom looked at me even more sharply. She stared at me with an instinct, one that God had deposited abundantly in all mothers.

Mom: *Yaake? Yaar hathraano saala maadidhre, kochch bidtheeni!*

(Why? If you have borrowed money from anyone, I'll pound you!)

The irony stung me. Here I was killing myself for months to save and mom assumed that I owed money. I quickly withdrew the emotions from my voice and body language. Twenty minutes later, Sriram and I were sitting and having breakfast at home. The Gayathri Bhavan dosas normally tasted delicious but today, they had no soul. With each bite, I was giving up a tick on my card.

A couple of months passed, and I made limping progress to the fourth column. At various points, I felt that so much struggle for so little money wasn't worth it. Additionally, a wayward instinct told me that the day I finally got my hands on the pile, I would spend it on something trivial. The journey would take so long that I would be totally spent. I wouldn't have the sense, energy or the excitement to put it to good use. A deep realization about money dawned on me: *Time and money have an intricate connection. If you make small money quickly, it's good. If you make big money within a short span of time, it's even better. But if you make loads of it and take a lifetime, it's pointless.* I decided to try and speed through my card. So, I started looking out for money wherever I could. Dad's pant pockets were the first thing that came to mind but I just couldn't do that. This act made me think at least twenty times and hence was too tiresome. There had to be easier ways.

A couple of weeks later, we visited the Raghavendra Swami Mutt. It was the festive season. As the *aarti* was happening, mom opened her little purse and took out some coins. She handed me ten paise to drop it into the plate when the pujari came around. I decided that I'd pretend to drop the coin but hold it back. The pujari stepped down from the elevated sanctum-sanctorum. He made his way slowly past the thronging crowd and soon, stood before us. Mom held my hand and extended it over the *aarti* plate. She would know if I dropped the coin or not. So, I opened my fist. Mom was getting in the way each time. With such rotten luck, I would never complete the card. I grew desperate and irritated. As I lifted my palms to my eyes to take in God's blessings, I prayed to Him to somehow give me the money. I assured Him that I was doing a worthy thing.

As soon as the *aarti* was over, people started ambling inside the huge temple hall. Lunch was to be served in twenty-five minutes. Different families and groups went to different corners of the hall and made little piles of their bags and belongings. Kids started running around and making a lot more noise. Most of the oldies had started settling down in their respective spots. The assistant pujaris were briskly handing out the consecrated offerings to the devotees. They stood atop a large, raised platform and kept placing trays at the edge of it. Each tray had a split coconut, a bunch of bananas, a few betel leaves, betel nuts and a length of jasmine flowers. Representatives from various groups rushed to the platform to pick theirs. I was randomly walking alongside the platform when I noticed a one-rupee note in one of the trays. The pujari had missed this offering to God and had placed the tray back with the money in it. This usually never happened. It had to be God's way of telling me that He had heard my prayers.

An hour later, we were back home. With three kilos of temple food in my stomach, I passed out. At five in the evening, I was at Mandanna's store. As he pulled out my yellow card, I pulled out the folded one-rupee note. He stared at me, and I thought I saw suspicion in his eyes. I told him that my grandparents from Bangalore had visited us for *Sankranti,* and added a small falsehood that my grandfather was very rich. He lowered his gaze to my card. After a brief mental calculation, he just drew vertical lines down the remaining columns. I had ended the match with a huge sixer. He kept his twenty-five paise and handed me two rupees fifty paise. I bought five *botis* and five peppermints. I handed back two rupees to him and said, `Red Card'.

. . . .

(9)

GIDDI'S DILEMMA

Giddi was my railway quarters' neighbour, not next door but five houses away. His dad and my dad were both railway guards and had been colleagues for over 13 years. They shared a bond so close that both families were one with four houses in between. In the rare event that mom and dad had to go out of town, leaving Sriram and me behind, we would eat at Giddi's house, hang around there and come home to sleep. Needless to add, the reverse was also true. Giddi and I were in the same class and therefore shared much in common. We enjoyed many similarities but a big difference was that I stood tall over Giddi. By any means, I wasn't big for my age but Giddi was stunted. In Kannada, Giddi means `shorty'. We were in class VII and going by his appearance, Giddi looked like a class III or IV student. Possibly because of this, I was the *guru* and he, the *shishya*, in all matters. Giddi was my ally in most schemes and didn't dare refuse any command, however batty it was.

It was February 1984 and class VII was an important year for us. My brother was in class X and his exams were even more significant. Sadly, my grandfather in Delhi expired and mom had to rush there. She would be gone for three weeks. Dad would keep going off on his train duty, some day trips and a few overnight ones. And so, with precise orders that Sriram and I were not to kill each other, mom departed. Dad left for work the next morning at six and his train would be back late in the

45

evening. Mom would have barely crossed into Andhra Pradesh when Sriram and I had our first fight, on flimsy grounds as usual. Both of us were studying and to break the monotony, I went to the kitchen to help myself to a handful of groundnuts. I turned around and saw him standing with hands on his hips.

Sriram: Oye! Kadlekaaye waste maadbeda. Vaapas bottle-ge haaku!

(Oye! Don't waste the groundnuts. Put them back in the bottle.)

I was ready to bite his ear off. This holier-than-thou attitude of his annoyed me no end. At the tender age of fifteen, he approached life with the gravity of a 48-year-old coal mine worker. I shot back, hissing like an angry cobra.

Me: *Naanu thintha idheeni, waste maadthilla. Harko!*

(I am eating, not wasting. Get lost!)

He grabbed my wrist, wrested open my fist, took away all the groundnuts, put them back in the bottle and ordered me out of the kitchen. Shouting Kannada abuses commensurate with my age, I swung my right hand at him. He held it, twisted my arm and whacked me on my face with a punch that landed below my left jaw. The helplessness stung far more than the blow. In my twelve years, this was the 538th fight that I had lost. He sagely marched out of the kitchen and went back to his books. I lay there sobbing at the wretchedness of my existence; I couldn't even enjoy a few groundnuts in my own home. On this particular day, something came over me. I decided that this was the last straw. As I pulled myself up, I decided to run away from home.

It was 12:30 in the afternoon and we had to go across to Giddi's house for lunch. I composed myself and headed there early. At the stroke of one, Sriram, Giddi and I had lunch in silence and then Sriram went home while I stayed behind. Giddi's mom cleared up the utensils and lay down for her siesta. The two of us went up the guava tree in his backyard. fter five minutes of random conversation, I suddenly declared with the bravado of Genghis Khan,

Me: *Giddi, naanu mane bittu od hog thidheeni.*

(Giddi, I am running away from home.)

Giddi searched my face long and hard to figure out whether

I was serious. I continued eating a semi-ripe guava. Seeing my resolve, he began to sob uncontrollably. I had a situation on my hands. I shook him, asking him to get a grip on himself.

Giddi: *Unf! pleeease hogbeda…unf…nanige yenu artha agthilla!*

(Unf! Please don't go…unf…nothing is making sense to me!)

Me: *Avanan magandhu gaanchali saakaythu. Tension beda. Yella plan maadidheeni.*

(I am tired of that scoundrel's highhandedness. You don't stress. I've got everything planned.)

Giddi's sniffles reduced. My confidence calmed his fear. He waited for the rest of the scheme.

Giddi: *Dabba! Yelli irthya?*

(Where will you live?)

Me: *Pumpset.*

The railway station was right behind our row of houses. Past the loco shed and the last shunting tracks, the wilderness began. There were irregular cattle tracks, an odd *jamun* tree and unfamiliar shrubs. Roughly half a kilometer into this wasteland was a patch of water called the pumpset. Water flowed over a long cement platform and formed a small pond, surrounded by squishy mud. Unknown to every parent, most children in the railway quarters took their first shot at learning to swim, in the pumpset. In fact, most parents forbade their kids from venturing beyond the tracks. Only the notorious and the most adventurous went there to prove their adulthood. Over a period of time, even decent kids like us had started splashing here. This was reserved mostly for the weekends. We would walk alongside the tracks for about 200 metres and at a particular point, turn right, walk through shrubs till the first sight of the pumpset made us charge towards it. Sometimes, when we did a late afternoon trip and hung around there till sunset, water snakes emerged around the periphery and hastened our departure. Giddi looked incredulous.

Giddi: *Dabba, yen heltha idheeya!*

(Dabba, what are you saying!)

I calmed him further.

Me: *Giddi, pumpset alli oota, neeru ide. Snana maad theeni, batte vogi*

theeni, hann sigathe, pakshi hodkond thin theeni…yenu thondre illa.
(Giddi, the pumpset has food and water. I'll bathe, wash clothes, have fruits, hunt birds…nothing to worry about.)

The pumpset was more than generous except for two things. One problem would be getting hold of fresh clothes. I had that worked out. At one end of our row of houses where the quarters ended and the forbidden wilderness began, was a petty shop. It sold bidis, cheap filterless cigarettes, basic vegetables, toiletries and other essentials. I told Giddi that once a month, I would have a rendezvous with him a little beyond this shop. Giddi was to supply me with a fresh t-shirt and a pair of shorts. Though still unsure how this would pan out, it was a concrete plan, nonetheless. One thing was sorted. The other is what gave birth to his dilemma. If I had to survive on fruits and birds, I had to have a knife. So, I ordered Giddi to get me the knife from the kitchen as I had no plans of going back home. Most kitchens had just one knife. If it ever went missing, the mother would look around for a few minutes in case she had misplaced it and then yell out the son's name. There were simply no other possibilities. Giddi knew very well that I had planned my flight at 7 in the evening. At 7:30 pm, his mom would enter the kitchen to cook dinner and at 7:34, yell out his name. He would then get prosecuted on two counts, for handing over the only knife to me and for being an accomplice in my daring escapade. Giddi was caught between two closing railway tracks. He started sobbing so vigorously that the guava tree began to shake.

Giddi: *Please Dabba…unf….hooo…chaaku maatra kodak aagalla.*
(Please Dabba...unf...hooo...I can't give you the knife.)

I had not expected his petty mindedness. Dripping with scorn,

Me: *Thoo! Naanu mane bit hogtha idheeni, ondhu putkaasi chaaku kodalva?*
(Shameful! I am running away from home and you won't give me a cheesy knife?)

I heard louder sobs.

Me: *Irli. Naan manage maadko theeni but friendship yenu antha ivathu gothaaythu.*

(It's okay. I'll manage but today I've understood the true worth of our friendship.)

Giddi started howling. I plucked another guava and looked into the distance. I had no reason to show pity towards him. Anyway, the sun started setting and with it, our states of angst and distress. Giddi gave me a used Ashoka blade from his dad's shaving kit, a length of nylon string and a box of Devi matchsticks. I also had my *chatribill* (a catapult made of highly tensile railway rubber, not bicycle tube.) One could easily down a bird on a high wire or a tree with one shot, not to mention mangoes, guavas, tamarind and other fruits. Even from a fair distance, it could easily deface a guy for life. As cartridges, we used handpicked stones and sometimes, pieces of iron.

In no time, it was dark. I braced myself to walk away from civilization. After a final hug and a reassuring hand on Giddi's shoulder, I walked out of his house. Walking past mine, I caught a glimpse of Sriram mugging mindlessly for his exams. With a final glance at the house that I had sworn not to return to, I moved on. Five minutes later, I had crossed Nayyar's Tailoring Shop. This marked the end of the railway quarters in this direction. For the first time since morning, I was all vacuum and panic effortlessly slipped into it. I had no idea what to do or where to go. Heading to the pumpset at this time felt impossible. It would have to wait till morning. And the night had just begun. Giddi's spirit probably entered me and I started sobbing, loud enough for few passers-by to take notice.

In my delirious state, I could think of only one name. Omi was the son of the maidservant who worked at my friend Vishak's house. Vishak's dad was a doctor and they lived in a big bungalow that I had just passed. Omi used to drop in once in a while to meet his mother and all of us always vied to get a piece of him. Omi was about eighteen, handsome with shoulder -length hair, practised karate and had developed a hoot of a tale he called Modern Ramayana, the epic but with Kannada film songs thrown in. If all of us had been granted the wish to be reborn as anyone else, we would have all been `Omi'. He worked as a waiter at the Chandrika Hotel, next to Shimoga City Club. In the growing darkness, I made my way there, alternately sobbing and howling. It was 8 o'clock and the hotel was buzzing with people in bush-shirts catching up on their day's proceedings over plates of *bondas* and filter coffee. I saw Omi come out of the kitchen with a tray of order. Like all waiters, he was in a white shirt. He looked like Karate Kid, abundantly more dashing than everyone else present. Omi saw me in the same instant and stopped in his tracks. He served his order, quickly said something to the manager and dragged me into the smaller Family Room.

Omi: *Ill yen maadthidya? Ella ok na?*

(What are you doing here? Is everything okay?)

Me: *Mane bittu od bandh bitte. Nin room alle irtheeni. Nanige waiter kelsa kodsu.*

(I've run away from home. I'll stay in your room. Get me a job as a waiter.)

Omi smiled. He said that this was no joke and that I couldn't stay with him as he himself didn't have a room. I was already at breaking point and retorted that I would go elsewhere if he didn't want to help me. As I turned away, Omi caught my arm and sat me down. He ordered me to stay put, dashed inside and came out with a plate of *chow chow baath* (a serving of upma and sheera) and a glass of hot badam milk.

As I was tucking into my tiffin, back in the railway quarters, Giddi had started sobbing again. It was nearly 8:30 pm and time for dinner. Sriram had gone across to Giddi's house and noticed my absence. When he enquired, Giddi tried hard to focus on his geometry textbook and casually remarked that he had no idea about my whereabouts. Within seconds, a casual enquiry turned into a matter of concern. Giddi's dad walked in from Nayyar's Tailoring Shop, which is where the fathers hung around when they were off duty. He was promptly informed. He yanked the geometry textbook from Giddi's hands and glowered at him. That's when the sobbing re-started. After feebly trying to deny any knowledge, Giddi confessed that I had run away from home. Beyond this, even he had no idea where I was. Dinnertime became panic time. Where could a 12-year-old vanish in the growing darkness? Giddi's dad and Sriram combed the vicinity. It was nearly nine and my dad's train was scheduled to arrive soon. Tensely, Giddi's dad and Sriram walked to the RPF Room. It was a one-storeyed brick building right next to the entrance of the railway station. The Railway Protection Force had two constables to take care of minor misdemeanours such as ticketless travel, pilfering and petty pickpocketing. They knew most of us, and all of us knew them as 'police uncles'. Two of them joined the search party and all four spread out in different directions.

I was done with my tiffin. Meanwhile, Omi must have sought the manager's permission to be relieved 30 minutes earlier. He took my hand and started walking me home. By now, the fight in me had vanished and I tamely let him lead me. In a comforting voice, Omi started telling me about life's challenges, how I still had years to grow up and that I should study hard and never think of running away. We were passing an auditorium and a Kannada play was about to begin. There was a line of people going in and a man at the entrance was hollering about the wittiness of the play into a megaphone. Omi suggested that we watch the play and he would drop me home after that. Now, I panicked. Since I had already decided to return home, my stress was of a different kind altogether. It was nearly 9:30 pm and we would take another fifteen minutes to reach home. It was a matter of shame and horror that any decent Kannadiga kid could be out on his own, so late. If we went for the play, I wouldn't get home before midnight. That would end up wiping out the honour of my entire lineage. More imminently, I wanted to hide in bed before dad got home. After such a wracked-out day, I didn't have the stomach to face him. I quickly dismissed the idea and insisted that we head home as quickly as possible. Omi was perhaps secretly relieved, and we continued our trudge.

As we approached the mouth of my lane, instinct told me that dad was home. I quickly thanked Omi and asked him to turn back. Omi looked at me queerly and insisted that he would see me into the house. He suddenly had doubts about my intention and thought that I might try and scoot again. I started to panic. If Omi accompanied me into the house, dad would know his background. And the fact that his 12-year-old son was friendly with an 18-year-old waiter would destroy him forever. In the eyes of the world as well as his own, he would be a failed dad. I pleaded with Omi to turn back, promising him that I would enter the house and that he be assured. I don't know if Omi read my mind but he listened to me.

I tiptoed to the door and stepped in. My sobbing had started again, against my will. I was truly sick of it by now. Dad, Sriram, Giddi, Giddi's dad and one police uncle were sitting around the room, looking terribly solemn. Either they were praying, or mourning. I ran straight into our only bedroom, jumped on the bed and covered myself with a blanket. I told myself to keep my eyes closed no matter what. I wanted to do the same with my ears. Pretty soon, the search party left. I sensed dad come in and switch off the light. Minutes later, I was out.

I got up at seven the next morning. I had been awake since six wondering how to face dad. I brushed my teeth and feeling like a worm, walked into our little kitchen. Dad was making coffee. I started sobbing (the last time in this story, I promise.) I prostrated at dad's feet saying 'sorry' multiple times. The cooking counter was to the left and in the right corner, at floor level, was a rectangular hollow space. It was the size of a television set. This was our puja corner. It had little idols of Lord Ganesha, Lord Narasimha (our family deity) and a couple of others. Like most people, dad was a religious, god-fearing man. He looked down and saw me at his feet.

Dad: *Ananda, ill alla, alli!*

(Not here, there!)

And pointed at the Gods.

. . . .

(10)

PANIC ATTACKS

I am not talking about fear. That's far more logical. Panic, on the other hand, is quite inexplicable. It's weird how over the years, some kinds of panic stay with you, some exit graciously as new ones seize you. As a kid, reptiles didn't bother me. I didn't like them but was at ease around them. As I grew up, the sight of a gecko would send a shiver down my spine. If I was put in a room with three of them, I became Nana Patekar in Parinda. But I never suffered from the panic that affects a lot of children: exams. They were more like pets to me; I played around with them. And since I helped out my classmates with their lessons and homework, some of them indulged me by either lending or giving me fancy things.

I was in the second standard and Sundar had got a rubber lizard to class. It looked so real that his dad had surely bought it on a trip to a bigger city. It was constantly being tossed around and most of us had a blast while a lot of the girls screamed. It was a big high. As the day came to an end, I asked him if I could borrow the lizard overnight. It was his first day with the new toy and ordinarily, he wouldn't have parted with it. But since I regularly helped him with his lessons, Sundar lent it to me quite easily. I wanted to show it off among the boys in the railway quarters. I entered home with the lizard in my hand. It felt yucky but nice. I crossed the drawing room and stood at the entrance to the kitchen on the right. It was the beginning of the month and mom was sitting on the floor, cleaning a plate of uncooked rice. On the first of every month, dad bought five kilos from the ration shop. The rice always carried visible signs of adulteration. In the first few days, mom would take portions of it on a largish round plate and do the needful. She looked up and went back to the plate. Without even thinking, I bent down and slid the lizard towards her. She screeched like a banshee and lunged up. The plate went flying in the air and created a little rainfall of rice. The cement gas counter was to her right and it's only providence that she didn't crash into it. Seeing her reaction, I froze. Panic spreads panic and I can't tell you whose heart was closer to a collapse. I had never seen her so scared and angry. I can't describe what she looked like. She slapped me hard but that didn't even register. The minute the lizard had left my hand, I had realized the folly of it. The rest had taken place within seconds.

Me: *Sorry amma, sorry, sorry, amma? ammaaa? Sorry, sorry…*

Extreme anger can only produce silence and mom just stood there panting hard. I couldn't face her and the silence anymore. Nervously, I went to the bathroom to wash my feet. My hands were shaking as I poured water with the plastic mug. Meanwhile, she had gathered herself, pulled out the broom and leaning away from it, swept the lizard out of the house. I came back to see her gathering the rice on the floor. The lizard was gone. Now I panicked. It was a brand new, unusual toy and not found in Shimoga. I was seriously answerable. At the same time, it was cruel to ask mom about its whereabouts. But I also realized that she couldn't have swept it out of the railway quarters. I apologized once more and meekly told her that I was heading out to play. She still said nothing. I met Giddi and the others.

Giddi: *Gultoriya?*

Gultoriya was a time pass game that we regularly indulged in.
Me: Lizard first!
We found it within twenty minutes.

However, the one thing that instantly turned me into putty was `injections'. Every year, around June or July, the railway hospital carried out a round of vaccinations for malaria. The area would get infested with mosquitoes, and it was already infested with pigs. Over a couple of weekends, two compounders from the hospital would go around poking people. Different rows of houses got different dates and timings. Like news of an advancing army, the panic would precede their arrival. You could hear the wail of a kid five houses away and knew that you only had half an hour to get away. Panic drove kids into water drums. In many houses, kids had to be dragged from under a Godrej almirah. Till date, no one knows how they fit under there. The compounders usually arrived at our doorstep with a 40-minute delay because of the above. The area had a sizeable population of panicky kids and if there ever was an election for President of Panic, I would have scored a landslide victory. On the day I had to get poked, dad casually told me that he wanted me around and that I should not step out. That was enough of a give-away because the railway quarters' drums had already started beating. Three hours before my appointed time, I began to insist that I would never get malaria and should be spared. Dad was usually more mild-mannered than a drop of dew. Even the mildest form of coercion was a huge ask of him. But now he goaded himself and threatened me that if I didn't comply, he would stop talking to me. At my age, this created panic of a different kind. Bouncing off for hours between two walls of panic (one triggered by my fear of the injection, the other by the fear of dad's punishment), I was a wreck. I tried to fill myself with courage but within seconds, it would seep out. It was like trying to hold a fistful of water.

When the compounders were two houses away, the four of

us were sitting in the living room waiting our turn. Mom and dad were parents and so they had to be composed. Sriram was only three years older and had to be closer to the panic line. I searched his face for signs similar to mine. But he had that faraway look. Even on a day like this, he wouldn't get his mind off the Milky Way and no earthly thing bothered him. He wasn't into cosmology; it's just that in my head, he belonged to a different planet. At 11:30 am, they were next door. In spite of mom and dad alternating between threats and allaying my fears, I lost my nerve. I darted out of the drawing room and went into the toilet. Before they could react, I bolted myself inside. The railway quarters' toilets were a little bigger than a 260-litre fridge. After ten minutes, the discomfort started growing exponentially. The compounders were almost at the door and this would now turn into a matter of shameful upbringing.

Compounder 1: *Subbarao-ge magan mele yenu control illa.*

(Subbarao has no control over his son.)

Subbarao was dad's name. The above dialogue was what my dad would imagine one compounder telling the other, later. Dad was enormously capable of such woeful imagination. So, mom and dad employed every ruse they could think of. They coaxed, threatened and ridiculed me; praised my common sense and tried bribing me with *raspuri* mangoes but nothing worked. They then moved from the subject to the object. They ridiculed, demeaned, debased, mocked and forcefully laughed at the injection. *Ha ha ha ha ha! Injection! Ha ha ha ha!* None of it made a difference. The fear of the injection was too powerful. I responded with silence. The compounders arrived and waited for ten minutes before their patience started wearing thin. There were five more houses in the direction they were headed before they had to veer off to another row. They offered dad a concession of 30 minutes, telling him that if he managed to get me out within that time, they would come back. I knew this, and also the next ruse that would crop up.

After leaving me undisturbed for ten minutes, mom and dad

slowly filled the house with sounds of gaiety. Some utensils jangled in the kitchen, mom loudly announced that we would have papads at lunch, dad called out to Sriram to go and get some juicy jackfruit, the radio was turned on and popular Kannada songs drifted around. All these were meant to send me signals that the murderers had left and life was back to normal and cheer. I was no fool. I knew that if I fell prey to this make-belief and stepped out, I would be pounced upon, wrestled down and terminated. So, I found comfort in the growing discomfort of the toilet. A couple of times, dad and mom sent Sriram to the latrine. He knocked on the door in desperation. I had no way of knowing if the plea was real or a trick. So, I took no chances. If he or anyone else had to genuinely use the toilet, they had to knock on the neighbour's door. I also knew that by late afternoon, the assassins usually ran out of serum for the day and retired. I finally stepped out a little after four. No one spoke to me for the next three hours but I had grown used to hours of silence by then. It wasn't such a big deal.

. . . .

SECRET FOUR

It was 1981 and it turned out to be a watershed year in our lives. We had started our fourth standard. Vishak and I were in the same class but weren't friends at first. That year, his parents built a big bungalow ten minutes from home and moved in. I had to go past his house on my way to school. Naturally, we got acquainted and grew close in no time. Pretty soon, this house became our hangout. Vishak, Amogha, Niju, Giddi, a few others and I spent most of our evenings playing here. It was a large house with a big compound all around, and a big terrace. The only small thing other than Giddi was Jimmy, a brown dachshund. None of us had ever owned dogs and this was a huge delight. Jimmy became the focal point of our existence. We even gave cricket the short shrift and spent every evening playing an assortment of games with Jimmy.

A few months into this blissful life, we came back from school one day and discovered that Jimmy had disappeared. This was unfathomable. There was no way the dog could have run away after five years with them. In all likelihood, it had been stolen. This was also weird as it was a dog and not a cycle. The house had a large side-gate towards the back for the Ambassador car to get in and out. The house faced a big road and on one side was a smaller lane that went down to a lowbrow neighbourhood. The other side had a large tract of empty land. The bungalow had no adjoining houses and stood majestically alone. Through the day, Vishak's mom was busy with her chores inside. Jimmy used to spend hours within the compound, bumming around. Given the nature and reputation of the surrounding area, it was quite possible that someone had managed to get away with Jimmy. We were devastated and went crazy trying to find him. For days, we cycled around in every direction after school, in the hope of spotting Jimmy. Vishak's dad, a doctor, did the same on his Vespa. After about a week, we lost all hope and went through a period of mourning. We would come back from school, change, head to Vishak's house and sit there till seven and not play. We even thought of announcing a 'Finder's Fee' but didn't go through with it.

Two months later, we wrote our mid-term exams and each of us went wherever one had to go for his holidays. On the first day of school re-opening, we all had stories to narrate but Niju had come back with the greatest piece of news.

Niju: *Vishak, Dabba, Amogha…Jimmy nodudhno.*

(Vishak, Dabba, Amogha…I saw Jimmy.)

We stared at him as if he had seen God. The four of us were standing in a circle and if we had tails, we would have caused muscle injuries with our wagging.

Me: *Elli? Saayankala hogi karkondu barona.*

(Where? We'll fetch him back in the evening.)

Two weeks earlier, Niju was on his way to a town smaller than Shimoga, to visit his aunt during the holidays. Travelling in a local bus, he was still very much within Shimoga limits when he spotted a brown dachshund in a huge bungalow. Niju said that though he had had a fleeting glimpse, he was convinced that that was Jimmy. The dog was of the same height, length and colour. He added that he wanted to jump off the bus right then but didn't know what he would tell his aunt who was waiting for him. We couldn't wait for school to get over.

At five in the evening, we were at Vishak's house planning a rescue. I thought about it and realized that we needed two things: a blade to cut its leash if it came to that, and our leash to bring it back. Vishak's dad regularly received promotional products from medical companies. Vishak remembered a fancy blade that his dad had around at home. It was a plastic box, about the size of a matchbox but much slimmer. The blade slid out from the side. Armed with this and our old leash, the four of us started from home. Since we had to walk back with Jimmy, we decided to leave our cycles behind. The place we were headed to was about two kilometres from Vishak's house. When we got there, Niju pointed out where Jimmy was being held captive. Facing the busy Savalanga main road was a row of big bungalows and Jimmy was in one of them. This bungalow was bigger than Vishak's and so, the owners had to be very rich. Why on earth would they steal our dog instead of buying their own? Anyway, that was for later. Luckily, the bungalow had an open site on one side and we could make a lateral approach. The four of us crept up to the compound wall and peered over it. Niju had been dead right. Lying down in a corner of that large compound was a brown dachy that looked exactly like Jimmy.

Four of us: *Tch…tch…tch…Jimmy…Jimmy…tch…tch...*

Jimmy ran towards the compound wall and started barking furiously at us. We were convinced. But in its excitement, Jimmy was barking so loudly that someone would surely come out. The more we tried to hush Jimmy, the louder this cute idiot barked. So, we walked and stood a few metres away. We realized that rescuing Jimmy would be a challenging task. At least, we had tracked him down. We planned to head back and inform Vishak's dad. Sidling up to the gate, I whispered to the madly-barking Jimmy that we would be back for him. Feeling on top of the world, we turned back.

Vishak and I were walking ahead of Niju and Amogha. That's when Vishak first spoke to me about something called a novel. Till then, we had only been into comics. The previous week, his aunt had presented him with a book and Vishak was only a few chapters down. He said that the book was about a gang of kids called Secret Seven, and was quite similar to our own mystery and adventure. I booked the book and Vishak promised that he would lend it to me within a week. Late in the evening, when

Vishak heard his dad's Vespa, he ran to the gate and gave him the lowdown about Jimmy. His dad heard him in all earnestness and at some point, began to smile. Being a doctor, he offered a medical parallel. He told Vishak that there were many pills that looked the same in size, shape and colour but in fact were totally different. Vishak caught on but said that Jimmy had responded to us by barking. His dad comforted him saying that he would check this out the next day. If the dog indeed turned out to be Jimmy, he promised that we would have him back by lunch. We were the most excited bunch in Shimoga as we left for school the next morning. As soon as school broke for lunch, we ran to Vishak's dad's clinic, about a kilometre away. As promised, he had swung past the other bungalow and made enquiries on his way to work. He began slowly telling us that he hadn't slept the entire night and had been equally hopeful but unfortunately, the dog looked just like Jimmy but was not. It had turned out to be a she-Jimmy. To all of us, this was a gloomy end to Jimmy's chapter. After this, our emotional strings snapped pretty quickly and life moved on.

Vishak finished the book in three days and passed it to me. Each chapter sent my mind in a hundred different directions. It was a magical journey. After this, there was no stopping us. Since Vishak was the one with more resources, we looked to him to buy more. At every opportunity, he asked his parents and family for books. They complied happily and our lives changed dramatically. Sitting in Shimoga, we soon started reading what the world was reading. We got to know words and characters that the world was familiar with. Our vocabulary grew and so did our minds and imagination. After devouring a dozen books in a span of three months, a pattern emerged in my head. The Secret Seven gang was no different from us. They lived in a small town and went about their lives. But one of them would notice something unusual or chance upon a random happening and voilà! they would be in the thick of a mystery. If it could happen in their small town, it surely could, in ours. We only had to keep our ears and eyes open. The next morning, I shared my thoughts with the gang. They scratched their heads for a bit and nodded in agreement. And so, in the winter of 1981, the Secret Four was born.

The first thing on our agenda was to put together a detective kit. In no time, this was ready, elementary but good enough to start with. The idea was to keep adding to it as we moved along. Soon, a Bata shoe box was filled with an assortment of things. We had 2 glass slides for blood samples and small plastic pouches for hair samples. A 50g pack of Ponds talcum powder and a roll of transparent sticking tape made up our fingerprinting equipment. Vishak gathered a couple of old reading glasses from his granny as part of the make-up kit in case we had to change our appearance to tail someone. We hunted all over Shimoga and finally found a place that sold costumes and accessories for plays. We bought two moustaches. By itself, the spectacles or a moustache was a giveaway. But combined, they made us incognito. The bare essentials were already in place: notepads, a pair of scissors, a tweezer, surgical gloves, 5 different coloured hats and caps, a magnifying glass, candles and pencils with thick leads for secret writing, a bottle of tincture, a roll of bandage, a small torch and a case file to maintain dossiers.

Every evening after school, instead of wasting our lives playing cricket, we headed out looking for potential cases. The modus operandi was to ride doubles on two cycles. The ones in front sat with small notepads and pens, and we would cycle to Shivamurthy Circle, Nehru Road and other bustling places. Over the next hour, we would keenly observe people and if anyone was suspicious-looking or looking around suspiciously, we jotted down his description. We usually covered two locations in an evening. The next morning, we would scan Deccan Herald and Kannada Prabha for crime info. They carried regular news of thefts, burglaries, pickpocketing and other misdemeanours. We would note down the details (the scene of the crime, time of the crime, description of any suspects) and then compare it with our notes. If we felt there could be a connection, the idea was to exchange our notes with the police. And in the bargain, also get some of theirs. With two hunting parties, the criminal would have a near-zero chance of escape. The `day of our lives' would be when we would beat the cops to solving a mystery. Whenever this moment happened, we had decided that we would not allow the police or the journalists to reveal our names and photos in the papers. Shimoga could never know who the Secret Four were.

On our daily rounds, there was no shortage of suspicious looking characters. Soon enough, we had our notepads brimming with words and phrases. Some of the more common ones were: drooping moustache, of medium build, swarthy looking guy, shifty-eyed, walked with a shuffle, sparse or thinning hair, a scar running down his left cheek etc. To our relief and confidence, these were pretty much the words and phrases that Secret Seven also had. Criminals the world over, apparently looked and behaved in a similar fashion. A couple of weeks went by and nothing came our way, though we were doing a thorough job. Maybe the newspapers carried wrong information by way of hearsay. Anyway, the biggest requisite in this profession was patience, as it was in cattle grazing.

One day, as usual, we were at Shivamurthy Circle. Our eyes fell on two guys who looked like they would burgle every house in Shimoga, in the years to come. They were about fifteen, looked steam-engine black and strong, and had a meanness about them. Gorging on pani -puri, they looked around surveying the scene. At last, we had a case on our hands. They finished eating, mounted their cycles and took off. The tailing started. We had to maintain a safe distance of twenty feet and yet not lose them. Niju and Amogha were riding while Vishak and I started jotting furiously. Vishak and I had more words and phrases in our heads and hence the arrangement. The men were pedalling down Savalanga Road, the same one with the she-Jimmy bungalow. Inter-city buses plied frequently here, and we had to maintain a safe distance from those too. The suspects were going at a fair speed and suddenly they braked. It was unexpected and we came to a halt within eight feet of them. They looked back to check for traffic before crossing the road. Inadvertently, they spotted us. Our four heads looked in four different directions. I sneakily covered my notepad. All six of us crossed the road and picked up speed again. One of them looked back and this time his gaze stayed on us longer. Moving alongside his accomplice, he uttered something that made him also turn back and look at us.

Clearly, they had sighted us and were alarmed. They started cycling faster. We were equally high on adrenaline and within minutes, eaten up a couple of kilometres. In our single-minded pursuit we had lost sight of our route and before we realized, had cycled behind them into a dangerous neighbourhood. This bordered one end of the railway quarters and was not at all known for its civility. It regularly churned out reports of fights, domestic abuse and unrest. In our gusto, we had thrown all caution to the winds and now, we were right in their backyard. For the first time, we were scared. They braked hard, jumped off their cycles and in that instant, we realized that they would grab us. If that happened, being held hostage for a few months was a strong possibility. As they scrambled to put their cycles on stands and block us, we yelled at each other to cycle for our lives. Both Amogha and Niju had strong legs and in the nick of time, we whizzed past them. They yelled many things but at our speed, nothing was coherent. Amogha and Niju cycled so hard that their diaphragms were nearly dangling out of their mouths. After twenty minutes, we neared Vishak's house but didn't stop just in case they were following us now. We cycled through 4-5 different areas and finally wheezed back to our base. This had turned out to be an extremely close call.

We went up to the terrace and just kept staring at the orange sky diminishing rapidly in colour. For a while, not a word was spoken. Gradually, syllable-by-syllable, we surmised that Secret Seven hadn't faced danger of this magnitude ever. Surely, they also had been chased or captured, at times. But in their town, the bad guys at most yelled at the Secret Seven, scared them and let them go. In Shimoga, we were dealing with dark, mean guys. One was never sure what they were capable of. It left us badly shaken and we decided to lie low for a bit. A week later, all of us had strangely lost the stomach for detective work and happily

* * * * * * * * * * * * * * * * * *

(12)

TIP-TIP-TIPPING

I was eight years old and living the good life. Unlike many, I hardly had any school stress, being adept at studies, recitation, drawing and athletics. I wasn't surprised when I was made the class leader of Section III B. I was equally good at pranks, bending the rules, thinking up oddball schemes etc., and held my own with the last-benchers as much as with the marks-chasers. This put me high up in the pecking order. As goes the adage, one slip and the fall would make an equally big impact.

Our class had four rows with six benches and desks in each. Every bench was shared between a boy and a girl. The convent sisters decided this at the beginning of the term and it stayed through. Some years, they changed the combination after the mid-term exams. My part of the combination was a girl called Nagrathna Bhat and we were quite friendly. It wasn't anything special other than being totally at ease with each other. Between classes, we exchanged notes about a variety of things: summer holidays, families, our pet hates, neighbours, best friends, favourite dishes etc. We also assisted each other with notes, sharpeners and erasers whenever required. One day, we had finished the first two classes and had our customary 15-minute recess at 11:45 am. We then came back for the last class before lunch. Now, the world over as in Shimoga, recess was designed so that one could take in fresh air and also relieve oneself. But only the most pressed would diligently do the latter. That was a precious waste of about six minutes of playtime if one took into account the queue for the loo.

Just like any other day, our gang of boys played a multitude of games in quick succession during the break. The last class started and Linette Miss was teaching us science. About ten minutes into the class, my bladder started throbbing. I ignored it and focused harder on what Linette Miss was saying. It was only a matter of another thirty-five minutes. A few minutes later, it started throbbing more. Now, I couldn't focus on the class. Pressing my thighs tightly, I prayed for it to ease. The harder I prayed, the more persistent it became. What added to the situation was the convent rule and I knew it better than the rest. When you came off recess and raised your little finger, the teacher invariably refused to accommodate the request. The whole point of the recess was to empty our bladders and this meant that we had misused the free time. No-go. I was grappling with these thoughts when I felt the first drop leave its source deep within. I was in no state to think logically about the convent rules and was about to raise my little finger when I heard a voice from the back of the classroom. It was Kiran, fondly called Koji. His pinky was up as he said meekly,

Koji: *Excuse me Miss, can I please go, Miss?*

Linette Miss gave Koji a cold, hard stare and commanded him to wait till lunch break. My last straw of hope vanished. Now, there was no way she would allow me. Resigned to my fate, I fuelled every ounce of energy to stop the flow. I pressed my thighs together so hard that light could not have passed through them. My legs were twisting in any position that helped. Despite my massive resolve, the bladder won. First drop by drop, then parcels of eight drops at a time and finally a stream gushed forth tip-tip-tipping on the floor. Nagrathna Bhat was intently listening to Linette Miss. She never once looked sideways or down. The very next moment, she stood up and blurted,

Nagrathna Bhat: *Miss! Miss! Water is falling from somewhere.*
As the flow eased down below, the flow in my eyes rose. I ran out of the class, leaving a thin trail behind. I ran and ran and ran for a good three kilometres till I reached home. Mom opened the door and before she could ask me what the hell I was doing at home, I ran to the bath- room. I washed, changed, ran to my bed and lay there sobbing. With a gentle hand on my shoulder, she enquired about what had happened. I told her about the horrible incident adding that I had been soiled for life. I told her to look for a new school, preferably in a new town. She tried her best to console me and dismissed this as a part of growing up. I dismissed her saying I was already grown-up. Kindergarten was a distant three years in the past! Burying my face deep into the pillow, I tried my hardest to block out this nightmare. Nagrathna's naively stupid face refused to leave my mind. The school building, the classroom, the morning assembly, hundreds of juniors and seniors, teachers, the librarian, Fees Miss, Mother Superior Rodrigues and the tip-tip-tipping sound continued to torment me. My pillow started smelling of urine and I threw it on the floor. I pulled the musty blanket over my face, bit into my forearm and fell asleep. When I re-entered the world, it was late evening. Though it was a weekday, mom had fried a big quantity of papads for dinner. Big deal! How could papads compensate for this humiliation? I had them, anyway.

The next day being a Thursday, I would have to stand in front of the school assembly. Imagine that! Something like this wouldn't have gone unheralded around the school. Perhaps time would work its healing magic, so I made it clear to dad that I was taking the rest of the week off. It was left to him to meet Mother Superior and buy me time. I finally returned to school on Monday and thankfully not one person said anything about the incident or looked below my waist.

. . . .

(13)

SUMEET

He came home with so much fanfare and excitement that it was second only to Sriram's birth. We got him from Madras as he was cheaper there by sixty rupees. Since dad was a railway guard, the travel to and fro was free. It had been two years since mom and dad had first planned this. When he did finally come home, so did many of our neighbours. Everyone wanted to have a close look and touch him. They sang his praises and admired my mom for her decision. She beamed like a once-again mother in the June of 1982.

Sumeet was a mixer with an exalted social standing, the most eligible marital replacement for any housewife. He came with three bodies of different sizes and three attachments. One looked like a Vishnu Chakra, the other was a semi-octopus and the third had just two blades. This looked the least menacing. Long after the crowd left, the four of us were sitting in the drawing room. Dad read every word of the booklet, twice over. After this, Sriram read it once more and sounded a lot like dad except amateurish. Mom listened intently to every word, all three times. Two pages into the first reading my mind started wandering. I made a definitive choice between `instructions to operate a mixer' and Tintin comics. Sumeet was then packed up and stored away carefully.

Meanwhile, idlis, dosas and chutney happened regularly.

There was nothing wrong with the grinding stone and mom continued to use the old warrior. But when days passed and Sumeet continued to stay out of sight, dad started showing traces of impatience. One day, when mom was at the grinding stone yet again,

Dad: *Yenu…*

Yenu with a question mark is 'What?' and with three dots is 'So…'

Dad: *Sumeet idhe! Comfffortable aagi chutney maadu. Yaake rubtha idhiya?*

(We have Sumeet. Make chutney comfffortably. Why are you grinding?)

Mom said that Sumeet was brand new and that we had to go easy on him. She added that her body still had strength to grind and so it was fine. Dad shook his head with a mixture of admiration and incomprehension. But he persisted with his 'Yenu…' every time he saw her working the grinding stone. So finally, in the last week of June, Sumeet was unpacked again. It was a Sunday and chutney had to be made. The five of us stood in the kitchen. Mom's backhanded casualness while making chutney was gone. I usually heard her humming Mukesh's songs while grinding the spices. Now, her mood was alert and cautious as she switched between reading passages from the booklet and operating Sumeet. Sriram and I had been asked to step back. Mom and dad also distanced themselves from it as much as they could. Their outstretched hands held the lid down. Not since their marriage sixteen years earlier had they stood like this. After going through the cautious motions, breakfast was ready but delayed by thirteen minutes. This marvel of technology or our handling of it had taken up more time. Sitting on the floor and polishing off the idlis, each of us remarked that the chutney tasted better than usual. Cleaning up Sumeet took an additional twelve minutes as this had to be done with total vigilance. He was then gently wiped dry and put in his place. Over a couple of months, the delays started coming down. All of us grew used to him and Sriram was allowed to handle Sumeet but he was still out of bounds for me. We had moved from manual to mechanical and felt chuffed.

Perhaps the only downside was the intolerable noise that this fellow made. Sriram and I would put down our textbooks whenever he ran. All of us would stay silent for the length of his running since it was impossible to carry out any conversation. Making chutney had to be timed to either before or after dad's puja. Two years later, when we had Solidaire, Sumeet came out either before or after Chitrahaar.

SOLIDAIRE

After Sumeet, mom and dad had begun saving up again. The world had started throwing up newer things, quicker. In 1982, INSAT–1A redefined the evenings in many parts of India, including many homes in Shimoga. Sometime in 1984, the four of us were sitting in the drawing room after dinner. My mosquito kung fu days were long gone. Sriram and I were now big enough to participate in family decisions. Dad announced that we would buy a television over the weekend. I beamed and lit up the drawing room better than any television. For nearly two years, I had frequently heard people say, `I watched television for 2 aworse yesterday.' Finally, dad had spoken and now we were talking. All four of us wanted a colour television but that costed around nine thousand rupees, clearly out of our reach for a few more years. This option had been thought through and thrown out of the window. There was no revisiting it. So, while there was excitement around the topic, none of us were exactly bouncy. We discussed Uptron, Solidaire and Nicky Tasha. All of us took a few minutes to think about these names. Uptron and Nicky Tasha didn't tell us much. On the other hand, Solidaire came across as a monument. In the event of an earthquake (entirely hypothetical since Shimoga is not in a seismic zone), it seemed that Solidaire would continue working. It got all four votes.

That Sunday, mom, dad and Sriram headed to Nehru Road. I was desperate to go along but a small piece of logic stood in the way. The four of us along with Solidaire, wouldn't fit in an auto. Sriram was stronger and would be more useful. Since he was also older, dad had hesitantly agreed that Sriram could ride shotgun only on this occasion. They left at 5 pm saying they would be back by eight-thirty. I got down to cleaning the drawing room though mom had already done her best. I then paced around the room in every conceivable geometric pattern. The clock struck nine and there was still no sign of them. I wasn't the only one getting restless. Quite a few of our neighbours were also pacing up and down.

When the decision had been made a few days earlier, it had been conveyed to everyone around though mom and dad had instructed us to hold it back from the neighbours. I think they liked to spring surprises on them.

Dad: *Announcements yenu beda. Firstu barli. Aamele helidre aaythu.*

(No need for any announcements. Let it come first. We can break the news then.)

I had nodded but deep inside, I saw myself telling whoever I came in contact with. I didn't understand the logic of their thinking. The next morning, I had informed friends and neighbours.

Me: *Sunday manege yeno bartha idhe. Adhara hesru Solidairu…*

(Something is coming home on Sunday. It's called Solidaire…)

In the evening, when I was back from school, mom was chatting with the neighbour who remarked,

Neighbour: *Solidaire thogotha idheer anthe?*

(So, I heard you are buying a Solidaire?)

Mom gave me a quick, dirty look and replied vaguely,

Mom: *Yochne maadtha idheevi, nodona…*

(We are thinking about it, let' see…)

I stepped in saying, *'We've thought. We've discussed. We've decided. And we are buying it this Sunday. It's true.'* Mom always did this vague thing. Anyway, we weren't the first ones in the railway quarters to get one. There were a few sets around already, but we were the first in our row. This generated enough excitement.

Ten minutes past nine, I saw a small headlight and then heard the sound of the auto. This was it. Autos came here only on very special occasions. As it sputtered to a halt, three neighbours rushed out and five men (Sriram included) carried Solidaire into the house.

This ten- feet journey was accompanied by eight instructions: to be careful, to hold one end up, to shuffle a bit to the left and so on. By the time it was placed on our round table in the corner, there were eighteen people in the drawing room. Sriram and mom couldn't stop beaming. Dad looked relaxed though. After a few rounds of congratulations, people left. Our next-door neighbour offered to send us dinner since we would be engaged with Solidaire. Mom politely refused saying she had made extra during lunch. A bank heist wouldn't have been planned so thoroughly. Finally, it was only the five of us in the room, obviously counting Solidaire. We sat there looking at it. It had two sliding doors and a lock. The doors weren't heavy duty. Made of thin wooden slats, they slid away from each other vanishing into a groove around the corners. Each door also had a little knob to help us slide it. When they were slid-shut, we could lock it too. Suddenly, Sriram and dad started feeling their pockets. They looked at each other and for a wee bit, I saw alarm on their faces. In the same instant, they realized that mom had the key in her purse. They laughed with relief while mom fished it out. Sriram took the key and unlocked the television. Suddenly, they looked at each other in confusion. I looked at the three of them, even more confused.

Dad: *Idhu beda antha helidhvala? Aamele thogondwa?*

(Hadn't we decided against it? Did we buy it later?)

Sriram: *Salesman-ge clear aage heliddhe, beda antha.*

(I clearly remember telling the salesman that we don't need it.)

Mom pulled out the bill and exclaimed, 'We haven't been billed for it.' Sriram's joy knew no bounds. He excitedly added that while mom was paying the bill, he had asked the shop person to demonstrate it once more, that he must have forgotten to take it off and we had got it for free. Mom said that since he had refused to give us a discount, God had decided to give us one by way of this. Dad looked uneasy. I looked completely lost. Sriram jumped up gleefully to show me the point of their discussion. On top of the television screen was a plastic screen, with four small clasps to clip it on. Sriram expertly unclasped it and placed it on my lap. As I held it against the light, he stood smugly behaving like its inventor. The plastic screen was divided into seven patches of colours: red, green, blue, yellow, orange, pink and a lighter shade of green. The patches were irregular and bordered each other. For all those who couldn't yet afford a colour television, some genius had come up with this colour screen for an additional three hundred rupees. These three had taken an hour to zero in on the television set but had debated this screen for close to two hours. Finally, they had decided against it as they collectively felt that three hundred rupees for a poor plastic pretender was a stretch. But Lady Luck had handed it to us for free.

Dad: *Naale return maadbidona.*

(Let's return it tomorrow.)

Both mom and Sriram looked at him sharply.

Mom: *Yaake?*

(Why?)

Sriram: *Appa, irli. Kalthana yenu maadilla.*

(Dad, let it be. We haven't stolen it.)

The next day, mom got down to stitching a cover for Solidaire. On her next trip to the market, she promptly picked up a plastic vase with plastic flowers. At 6 pm every evening, like a cabaret joint, the shutter doors would be unlocked. A panel of four would start discussing farmers, pesticides, tractors and silkworms. This was the warm-up. The cabaret act started later when Chitrahaar began. Evenings were now spent regularly watching Jeetendra, Sridevi etc. followed by Salma Sultana, Tejeshwer Singh and other newsreaders, all divided among the seven colours.

After a few months, it became tedious and hurtful to the eye. One day, Sriram unclipped it. Watching Chitrahaar in black and white wasn't appealing to the eyes or the ego but we learnt to live with it. The plastic screen lay on top of the almirah for a few months till we sold it to someone in the railway quarters for eighty rupees.

· · · · · · · · · · · · · · · ·

(14)

RICHES TO RAGS

Mom thundered at me.

Mom: *Vayas eshtu?*

(How old are you?)

Eyes downcast, I answered with a mumble.

Me: *Entu vare, amma.*

(Eight and a half, mom.)

It was a ridiculous exchange between a mother and her son but the situation was grave. Her slap was still stinging my cheek and ringing in my ears. She had smacked me so hard that I stood like the Leaning Tower of Pisa.

Mom: *Appa manege barli. Straight remand home-ge haaktheevi.*

(Let dad come home. You are going straight to a remand home.)

As I silently prayed to every God, she impounded my life's earnings. With disdain writ large on her face, she pushed the plastic cover under the Godrej almirah. The fact that I had managed to keep my stash away from her sight for nearly a month, was in itself a miracle. The house wasn't large and mom regularly cleaned every nook. I had to take my stash out of the house and bring it back in, every day. Now finally, luck had betrayed me, and I stood facing my doomsday. Irrespective of the dire circumstances, I couldn't help but think gloriously about

Tikki. It had filled me with so much excitement and riches this particular Summer.

Tikki was a game that had always beckoned me but one that I hadn't been allowed to play till now. There was an unwritten code among the boys in the neighbourhood. The older boys in the railway quarters forbade the younger lot from playing until we reached a certain age. I had finally made the cut this year. *Tikki* was played with empty cigarette packs. Participating in a game required some work but it was exhilarating. First, I had to scavenge all over the railway quarters and collect discarded packs, tear out the two broad outer sides, place one on top of the other (one lengthwise and the other sidewise) and fold it into a small square called a *tikki*. What struck me as odd and exclusive was that *Tikki* was the only game where its name as well as its currency was called the same. I ran various games through my mind and not one conformed to this unique principle. The game had a capital 'T' and the currency, a small one. Nobody had ever put it down on paper but it always worked like this in our heads: 'Shall we play *Tikki*?' versus 'How many *tikkis* do you have?' Depending on the brand of cigarettes, each *tikki* was assigned its own value. No one knew who had decided but they were loosely based on the cost of the cigarettes and the ease with which the packs could be found in the dustbins.

Berkeley - 15

Scissors - 25

Bristol - 50

Navy Blue - 75

Wills - 100

Gold Flake - 125

These were the bourgeois *tikkis*. Kool, on the other hand, belonged to the cool category. It came in a green pack, wasn't freely found and therefore, carried a higher value of 300 points. But the ultimate was General. It looked a lot like Big Fun bubble gum wrapper, with alternating white and pink stripes. The General's pink was a lighter shade. Finding a pack of General was equivalent to unearthing a fossil and so the inventors of

Tikki had given it an exponential value of 1000 points. All of us went General-hunting in our spare moments. I would scavenge more than 20 dustbins and if lucky, come across one. The other essential to the game was a *jappa* (a round, flat, smooth stone) akin to a slice of cassatta ice cream. The game itself was simple but engrossing. We drew a huge circle on the ground and about 30 feet from it, drew a line. Then the stakes got decided. If it was 100 points per player, all the players put in their share of *tikkis* which got stacked in the middle of the circle. From the start line, the first guy slid his *jappa* on the ground towards the stack. Even if he missed it, his *jappa* would now be much closer to the stack of *tikkis*. The rest followed suit. Then the first guy got his turn to hit the stacked *tikkis* or the dislodged pile. If his *jappa* drove a *tikki* out of the circle, it was his. At the end of a game, some went home with hundreds or even thousands of currency while the rest went back to the dustbins. My debut season had turned out magnificently, almost on par with Michael Holding's 14 wickets for 149 runs. The boys called it Beginner's Luck. Whatever, but I had the riches. I had a portfolio of *tikkis* worth 5,400 including two Generals.

When dad entered, mom ranted with fury while I apologized with an equal amount of remorse. It was tough matching up to her though. Dad looked sapped midway. In an extremely distressed and uneasy voice, he muttered-uttered (some bits eaten up and some audible),

Dad: *Aiyo! Vamshana hesre haal maad bityallo!*
(Alas! You've ruined the reputation of our clan!)
I swore that I would never indulge in *Tikki*. Dad picked up my stash with disgust, mounted his cycle and returned after half an hour. I was sure he had gone to the farthest dustbin.

· · · · · · · · · · • • • • • · · · · · · ·

(15)

108 PROMISES

It was a typical railway quarters' Sunday. Giddi and I were playing marbles with Satish. He was of the same age but studied in a different school. His father was the Station Master, and they were Malayali Christians. They spoke a slightly different Kannada that sounded funny to us. Their food was vastly different as they ate meat. Giddi and I were brahmins and obviously our families looked upon non-vegetarian food, including eggs, as a curse. Let alone eating, we weren't supposed to see or even utter the words. Sometimes while chatting at home, if we accidentally said `chicken' or `mutton' or any other despicable word like that, our parents would bang their foreheads before banging our cheeks.

On Sundays, we ate what we normally ate through the week. But a lot of families who ate `those things' made `those dishes' specially on holidays. As we were nearing lunchtime, Satish licked his lips thinking of the treat waiting at home. When we enquired what it was, he mentioned that there was pork chilli for lunch. For some peculiar reason, Giddi and I felt the same thing in the very same instant. With a remote excitement and a lot of nervousness, I blurted,

Me: *Giddi, ondh ondh piece try maadona?*

(Shall we try a piece, apiece?)

Giddi: *Naanu adhe yochne maadtha idhdhe.*

(I was thinking the same.)

We had never had any craving or even a dull curiosity to sample anything non-vegetarian. Strangely, on this day, both of us

77

suddenly felt like doing the unthinkable. This was nothing but `Let's do the forbidden' syndrome. After that impulsive moment, we looked at each other with dread. This one came with so much risk that one slip of the tongue and we would be skinned alive and disowned. But we decided to do it anyway.

Me: *Giddi, yene aadhru yaarigu yaavathu helbaardhu! Promise?*

(Whatever happens, you'll never tell a soul! Promise?)

Me: *Amman aane?*

(Mother promise?)

Me: *Appan aane?*

(Father promise?)

Me: *Ajjan aane?*

(Grandfather promise?)

Me: *Ajji aane?*

(Grandmother promise?)

Me: *Devraane?*

(God promise?)

In return, he asked me the same. Over the next five minutes, both of us repeated this entire set, twice. We promised each other with absolute sincerity and conviction but somehow each round of promise made us ask the other for another. We then individually went through a round of promises with Satish. We walked into his house to the thudding sound of our heartbeats. The house was empty. His dad was at the station, mom was at the neighbour's place and his two younger brothers were somewhere in the neighbourhood. In all likelihood, they were chasing pigs. Those two had a strange fascination for rushing towards an unsuspecting pig and making it bolt in fright.

We entered the kitchen. Satish lifted the lid off the vessel. Giddi and I peered in and saw small chunks of dry, light brown pork garnished with chilli and grated coconut. Giddi asked me to go first. I reversed the offer. Either of us weren't ready to take first strike. Finally, we decided to do it simultaneously. We made one more set of promises and picked up a tiny piece each. We were now soiled for life. We held the pieces at the entrance of our wide, open mouths. They hadn't yet crossed over or touched anything other than our fingers. Giddi and I kept looking at each other diligently. A tiny piece of pork had created a huge amount of suspicion between two great friends. We lowered the pieces slowly to a few millimetres above our tongues, still eyeing each other.

Me: *Haan?*

Giddi: *Haan!*

The next instant, we committed the unthinkable. There was thunder, lightning and high tides. Storms raged and the earth cracked open in a few places. A hundred varieties of juicy fruits rotted in an instant. The temple bells clanged like they had lost their marbles. Electrical devices shut down and perfectly running trains screeched to a halt. Centuries of Brahminical fury was unleashed and it was destroying the world around us. But in Satish's kitchen, we heard none of it except deathly silence. Giddi and I had turned white with fright. I chewed twice and it felt tasteless, like rubber. Seconds later, we ran out of the kitchen into his backyard and spat it out. For precisely three seconds, Giddi and I had ceased to be brahmins. The excitement was over and done with, and so was the pre-anxiety. Now the post-stress kicked in and was as much, if not more. The `pre-' was about toying seriously with a filthy thought. The `post-' was about living the rest of our lives with this dreadful past. This also made us sitting ducks for anytime-anything-blackmail. The blackmail if ever, would cut both ways but it still made both of us feel extremely exposed. So, Giddi and I went through two more rounds of our 6-layered promises and individually again with Satish. Giddi started feeling giddy. I was also feeling lightheaded.

We decided to split and head to our respective homes. It was anyway close to lunchtime. That day, I emphatically told mom that her lunch was out of this world. Mom looked at me strangely because she had made standard fare. Clearly, my guilt was acting up. Over the next month or so, Giddi and I went through our round of promises every now and then. And we did the same with Satish too, especially after he would lose to us in a game of marbles. At some point soon after, we got over our dormant fear and life carried on.

. . . .

(16)

28 MONKEYS

Class VA had 43 students, with 15 girls. Someone had to monitor and I was appointed the class leader. A part of my morning duty was to stand at the door of the classroom to ensure that everyone was convent- worthy in all aspects: polished shoes, tied shoelaces, no missing buttons, no rebellious strands of hair, house badges in place etc. Each day came with a few violations that got sorted without much fuss.

It was a lovely morning in August. The rainy season had settled into a nice cadence after erring badly on both sides of its swing. All of us looked fresh and smelled nice, just like the campus ground. As soon as the assembly got over, I went ahead and stood outside our class door. As everyone trooped in, the day looked abnormally normal. Then my gaze fell on Avinash. He had a red welt where his nose met his forehead. For a moment, it looked like a *nama* (tika) but it wasn't. His skin was abraded and carried a red line about a centimetre long. Before I could ask, he had moved in. I noticed a similar mark on Shirish's forehead. Then Melvin, Amogha and Guppy walked in with similar welts. It showed alarmingly well on Guppy's forehead as he was fairer than the rest. *(His real name was Sumanth, and he had a big collection of fishes at home. He knew more about them than they themselves did. He fed them, bred them and regularly spread them across numerous tanks and aquariums at home. He had left us with no choice but to call him Guppy.)*

Pressy Miss entered before I could delve further into the mystery. As soon as the first period ended, I asked Avinash. All the scratched boys gathered around and exclaimed as if they had discovered Penicillin.

Scratched Boys: *Hanumantha barthaane.*

(Lord Hanuman will appear.)

We were of that age where the mind only took in headlines, and rarely went beyond. Instead of logically asking why and where the Lord would appear, I asked enthusiastically,

Me: *How?*

Avinash: *If you scratch yourself a 1000 times.*

Shirish: *I have already done 61 times.*

Amogha: *50*

Guppy: *38*

As was the case with most such schemes, no one knew who had started this or its authenticity. That morning, the first band of boys had been told of this miracle and they had already initiated Lord Hanuman's journey. Emilia Miss walked in and we scurried back to our benches. Over the next two classes, no lesson registered in anyone's head. Algebra and digestive systems seemed so trivial compared to a divine sighting. As the classes wore on, all of us started scratching. Of course, this had to be done with caution. Quite a few of us rested our chins on our palms and stared intently at the black board. In the process, we had also half-covered our faces like Manoj Kumar. Ever so stealthily, we kept adding to our tally of scratches. When we broke for lunch, all of us went nuts. We ate hurriedly, cancelled our lunchtime games and sat down with our forefingers and foreheads. Sitting in groups under various mango trees, we went into divine bliss. After about 40-50 scratch-es, the skin peeled, turned red and sore. Further scratching became extremely difficult and painful. The guys ahead in the race instructed the newcomers to take it easy. The right procedure was to give it a break for a few hours and then resume.

The afternoon classes started and all of us walked in feeling blessed to varying degrees. The girls looked at us with alarm and excitement. Some of them enquired about the welts and a couple of us shared the grand plan. The girls involuntarily touched their foreheads and cringed. They were more worried about their looks than meeting God. As the day ended, we gathered again for a while, scratched some more and headed home. In this second round, we couldn't add beyond 20- 30 scratches. The maximum tally on the first day stood at 127. When we had heard about it in the morning, all of us had felt that we would see Hanuman by the end of the day. Now, we realized that the target of 1000 would take days, maybe even weeks. After heading home, a lot of us smeared a little talcum powder to cover the mark. Anyway, the scars on day one weren't very pronounced and no parent noticed.

Day two began with more excitement. Some boys had reserved this activity only for school while others had raced ahead. They had added to their tally while lying in bed and walking to school. Shirish was close to 200. He was clearly the topper and beamed like one. Some of us were way behind and a little disturbing thought crossed my mind: Would Lord Hanuman appear only once, to the race winner or re-appear individually for each one of us? When the deal had been shared, this clause hadn't been spoken of. I checked with Avinash who checked with Shirish who asked Guppy who enquired with Melvin and we hit a dead end. We stopped scratching for a couple of hours till this became clearer. If there was only one appearance, it didn't make sense to carry on. During lunch, we discussed and reasoned. Lord Hanuman was one of the most selfless Gods and also the least busy. He always had time for odd things. So, we concluded that He would make a private appearance for each one of us. We resumed with vigour.

By day three, Lord Hanuman was still two-thirds of the way away. The race leader had barely touched 320. Progress had become painfully slow. The welts had become deep and dark. Now they couldn't be easily missed, especially when 28 boys with welts stood together in the assembly line or sat in class. Boys from other sections started enquiring, staring and talking about it. Gradually, our fear also turned deep and dark. The Mother Superior and the teachers had enough instances in a day to look at us and inspect us closely. If they ever found out, they would leave much deeper scars on our knuckles and the backs of our thighs. They only spoke about Jesus and would never get the bigness of Lord Hanuman. Not that they had anything against Hindu Gods but they had archaic convent rules. For instance, we couldn't hurt another person and that was understandable. But we also couldn't hurt ourselves, even if it was to invoke God. So, I alerted the gang to be extra cautious. Everyone was instructed to keep his head lowered a bit, at all times.

On the fourth day, in walked Emilia Miss. Something was amiss. She was supposed to conduct the second class and not be here at the beginning of the day. She was also the strictest of the teachers. From the corner of my eye, I took in the class to see if the heads were down. Emilia Miss held her head high as she surveyed the class.

Emilia Miss: *Anand, come up here!*

I realized the game was up. The authorities knew. As I slowly stood and walked up, I sent out a strong, silent prayer.

Me: *Lord Hanuman, please…either you appear or make us disappear!*

In this tense moment, I noticed another upsetting act. All the girls in class held their heads high just like Emilia Miss, and stared blankly straight ahead. This was to give an impression that they knew nothing about the plot; a classic posture of masking their knowledge about their devout brothers. I stood in front of Emilia Miss. My head wasn't lowered. It wasn't worthy of a class leader. He had to, at all times uphold intelligence, discipline, academic performance and his own head. Emilia Miss stared at my little doorway to Lord Hanuman. She then looked at the rest of the class. The boys moved their heads in various angles looking guilt-ridden and inept. Staring at my scar once more, she asked,

Emilia Miss: *Anand, what is this?*

Across the five subjects that we studied, I had answers to every question but not this. Divine topics were never questioned. They had answers but the explanation was always too elaborate and complex. My best option was to stay mum.

Emilia Miss: *All of you with a scar! Come to the front of the class!*

Not one boy moved.

Emilia Miss: *ALL OF YOU WITH A SCAR! COME TO THE*

FRONT OF THE CLASS!

With a slow shuffle, each boy inched forward. Within a few minutes, the shorts were staring at the skirts and vice versa. One sari was standing in the midst, fluttering with unjustified anger. The girls now became very self-conscious. They didn't want to look us in the eye. They also didn't want to lower their heads and become a part of collective guilt. So, they morphed into a confused herd: shifty, brazen, concerned, unaffected, motherly etc. In a random sequence, Emilia Miss barked at a few of us.

Emilia Miss: *How many times?*

Jayanth: *96 times, Miss.*

S P Arvind: *Only 37 times, Miss.*

Both of them had cheated by nearly 60 or 70. For a minute, it looked like she was out to get everyone's count. Our minds started racing, thinking of a false but believable number. She sat on her chair and picked up the ruler. Without any instruction, all of us fell into a line, almost straight. One by one, we walked up as she impassively cracked open the skin on our knuckles with the ruler. Each one got exactly six, three on each hand. Without making eye contact with any of the girls, we lowered our heads and went back to our seats. Emilia Miss walked out. Thirty-five minutes out of a forty-five-minute class had been taken up by this beastly act. Academics had suffered but the authorities didn't care.

At lunch, all the scarred boys grouped together once more. None of us had anything coherent or intelligent to say. Some were angry on religious grounds, some looked idiotic, some felt victimized for having been drawn into it and a few felt scared about Mother Superior calling their parents. I felt disappointment, confusion and more than a little anger towards Lord Hanuman. He surely had to know about this and if so, why the hell had he set it at 1000? He could have kept it to just 100; even 250 was manageable. No doubt He was great but ultimately, He was a monkey. He was playing stupid games with us and laughing at our expense. It was only ten days later that the last visible signs vanished fully and the class looked normal again.

· · · · · · · · · · · · · · · · · · · ·

(17)

BICYCLE THIEF SIR

At the edge of the railway quarters, immediately after KEB Circle, stood a row of shops. The first of them was Nayyar's Tailoring Shop. Nayyar was so hardworking that he hardly spoke. Maybe his father had advised him at a young age, *"Son, you'll reap what you sew."* And so, he barely said one sentence for every three shirts that he stitched. From ten in the morning till eight in the evening, he worked without expression except when he had to change bobbins. It was a small shop, a little larger than a railway guard's compartment. Because of this, all the railway guards hung around here in their spare time. Maybe they found comfort in a space that was similar in size to their workspace. With a slight stretch of imagination, the sound of the sewing machine was similar to that of a running train. And just like a train, the sewing machine also ran and stopped, ran and stopped. Nayyar had placed a wooden bench against a wall. It easily accommodated three people. Whenever the railway guards were off-duty and off home-duty, they met here. Most of them didn't speak much at home but at Nayyar's shop they were constantly talking. They had an endless run of topics to chew upon: school fees, prices of kerosene and firewood, Provident Fund, Dearness Allowance, academic performance of their kids, budget, state and national politics, Second Pay Commission, Railway Tribunal, fixed deposit rates and other subjects of existential importance.

A few shops to the right was Kuppa's Hair Cutting Saloon. Till I was thirteen, Nayyar stitched all my clothes and Kuppa cut all my hair. I wasn't the only cursed one. Most people in the railway quarters could lay claim to both of the above. Every forty days, dad went to Kuppa for his haircut. Once a month was ideal for him but that worked out a little expensive. By enduring the extra ten days of hair growth each time, he had managed to bring down the annual cuts from twelve to nine.

I was in the sixth standard and dad had hit his fortieth day of hair growth. He had finished his night duty and the day was his. More importantly, it was a Wednesday. We weren't supposed to cut our hair on Tuesdays and Thursdays. The logic for this was hard to find, scattered across the Vedas, Puranas, the Upanishads and so it made sense to skip those days than get to the bottom of it. So, at eight in the morning, he mounted his Raleigh cycle and went to Kuppa's saloon. He waited his turn by reading the Kannada Prabha supplement. Half an hour later, he stepped out looking his smartest. He felt the back and the sides of his head to ensure that all the unwanted locks were gone. Suddenly he stopped short. His cycle too was gone. Dad was given to forgetfulness and for a second, he wondered if he had come on the cycle, in the first place. He stepped in to reconfirm this with Kuppa. Kuppa's shop faced east and in the mornings, unnecessary sunlight barged in. Because of this, Kuppa had two curtains on the inside. He hadn't noticed if dad had brought his cycle or not. But eventually, dad clearly recollected having brought the cycle as well as locking it. His knees wobbled. Hawaii chappals stolen outside the Raghavendra Swami Mutt was understandable but a cycle outside Kuppa's shop? This had never happened in all these years. A God-fearing, middle-class Kannadiga brahmin never imagined that his house would get burgled or his cycle stolen. He was devastated and couldn't think straight. Praying and stressing, he walked home.

As he stepped inside, mom was waiting. She had readied a bucket of hot water and stood with the plastic mug in her hand. As brahmins, we could not touch anything right after a haircut, not even the mug and the bucket. Someone else at home had to first pour three mugs of water on the brahmin with freshly shorn hair, and then he could take over. Since Sriram and I were at school, mom was the mug-handler. She took one look at him and asked if things were fine. Dad had lost a lot of his colour. He was feeling so hopeless and helpless that he didn't answer.

Mom: *Yen aaythu? Heltheera?*

(What happened? Will you tell?)

Dad agonizingly told mom that their cycle had been stolen. Her hand started shaking as she poured water on dad's head. Dad finished his bath and sat down for his puja. For all his piety, he performed a very disturbed one. Meanwhile, mom was sitting in the living room brooding over our fate. They then ate *uppittu* (upma) in silence. By now, dad was filled with extreme guilt and could hardly make conversation. When we accidentally broke or lost something, we used to feel guilty. But we also felt equally guilty when someone stole something of ours. It was illogical but that's how it was. Maybe we had sinned at some point, God knows! Maybe one of us had stolen someone's tractor in our previous birth and now God was getting back at us.

Mom: *Yen maadona eega? Police hathra hogtheera?*

(What do we do now? Will you go to the police?)

Dad shook his head. A policeman never figured in any of our sacred texts (Gita, Ramayana, Mahabharatha, the Vedas etc.) and hence never figured in our lives as well. In fact, the purest life a brahmin could lead was one where he went through without ever coming in contact with the police. Still unsure of what to do, dad walked back to Kuppa's saloon, wildly expecting to sight the cycle. It betrayed his hope. He then walked the few steps to Nayyar's shop and sat down wearily on the bench. A couple of his colleagues were already there. Painfully, he recounted the doom. He didn't leave out a single detail including the article he had read in Kannada Prabha while waiting his turn. As he reached the climax, the other guards shook their heads with as much agony. For the first time in years, Nayyar stopped stitching for fifteen minutes until dad ended his narration. Over the next

two hours, three railway guards and one tailor did four things in a loop. They created parcels of silence, mumbled curses at the thief, shook their heads and discussed the facts of the case.
1. What was dad wearing?
2. Was his cycle parked to the right or left of the door?
3. What time had he left home?
4. How many people were present in Kuppa's shop?
5. How long had dad waited for his turn?
6. What article was he reading in Kannada Prabha?
This discussion wasn't for cracking the case though. It was a sort of brahminical penance, to live through the agony of the misfortune and thereby redeem oneself. Around lunchtime, everyone went home.

That afternoon, as they lay down on the straw mat for a nap, mom had already started working out a savings plan in her head. A new cycle cost Rs.650 and the quality definitely wasn't as good as the ones earlier. That wasn't in our control though. With each rotation, the world grew more inferior. A good, old cycle was gone and we would never ride one of that calibre again. She promised to try everything in her might to put this money together as soon as possible. Of course, that would still take 3-4 months. When we got home from school, Sriram and I heard about the incident. I seethed for a while. Then I exclaimed that we should buy an even superior cycle. That scoundrel would never strike us a second time and this would make him feel miserable that he had stolen the lesser of our two cycles. Mom, dad and Sriram looked at me strangely. Their logic always worked in a straight line.

Over the next two days, all the regulars in our lives heard about the incident. A few days later, dad was sitting in Nayyar's shop. It was evening and there were two people with him excluding Nayyar. All of a sudden, Babu barged into the shop. Babu was a cycle mechanic. He had his tiny shop in the same row as Nayyar's. What Nayyar was to our clothes and Kuppa to our hair, Babu was to our cycle. Since the beginning, he had fixed every puncture. He knew our cycle better than he knew his kids.

Gasping for breath, he exclaimed,

Babu: *Saar, nim cycle ille idhe!*

(Sir, your cycle is right here!)

The three guards creaked to a halt. Nayyar stopped stitching.

Dad: *Heng saadhya? Kalthana aaghoythu.*

(How is it possible? It got stolen.)

Babu: *Saar, nimdhe! Aa kal nan maga dose tintha kooth idhaane. Seatu, locku change maad bit idhaane.*

(Sir, yours only! That bloody thief is sitting and having dosas. He's changed the seat and the lock.)

Ten minutes earlier, Babu had taken a break and walked down to Gayathri Bhavan. He was standing outside and slurping tea when he saw a stranger arrive on a cycle. He parked it, went inside and ordered a plate of dosas. Babu threw one glance at this cycle and knew it belonged to us. He left his unfinished tea and had come running.

Slightly unsure but hugely hopeful, dad hurried across with Babu. They saw the cycle and it was indeed ours. Babu then stealthily pointed to the man having dosas. He was a big guy, not epic-big like those in the mythologies but much bigger than both dad and Babu. Dad felt hesitant to confront him. They had neither proof nor size. He could easily brush both of them aside and ride off. Plus, they didn't have enough time to call the police. The thief finished his dosas and started slurping on his cup of coffee. Dad told Babu to quickly fetch the other two railway guards. Babu ran to Nayyar's shop and came back running, along with dad's colleagues. With more strength in numbers, the four of them stood near the cycle. The thief got up, wiped his moustache and walked out. The Shaolin brothers blocked him. Actually, Babu was no pushover, but he was the second line of attack or defence depending on what played out. The opening belonged totally to dad.

Dad: *Saar, ee cycle nimdha?*

(Sir, is this cycle yours?)

The thief hesitated. He looked around for more Shaolins in hiding. Clearing his throat he said unsurely,

Thief: *Haudhu! Yaake?*
(Yes! Why?)
Dad: *Henge saar? Nimdhu henge? Idhu nandu.*
(How sir? How is it yours? It is mine.)
The thief paused, thought and said,
Thief: *Haudha? Seri, itkoli.*
(Is it? Ok, keep it.)
He strode away. The three guards lurched forward and held the cycle. Babu was aghast. In less than a minute, the thief had let go of the cycle and these three had let go of him. It was the most bizarre thief encounter anyone had ever witnessed. Perhaps it was also the only encounter where a thief was addressed as 'Sir'. Babu ran looking for him but the big guy had vanished in a trice. He ran back and said that they shouldn't have let go of the thief. Dad wasn't remotely interested in Babu's anguish. He was all 5 feet 5 inches of relief for getting his cycle back and for having the shortest, most pleasant thief-encounter. Dad lovingly touched every part of the cycle. The seat and the lock gave him the creeps. There was something sinful about them. He told Babu to change them the next day. As they walked back to Nayyar's shop, dad thanked Babu profusely and handed him a ten-rupee note. Babu took offence, not the money. Nayyar was equally thrilled. He looked up from the pant and thanked God in Malayalam. After discussing the bizarre case for thirty minutes, dad cycled home to tell mom news of our great fortune.

That evening, mom made payasa though it was a regular weekday. Over dinner, I told dad multiple times that he should have apprehended the thief. We could have then tied him to the cycle and dragged him all over the railway quarters. Dad shook his head in vain and said,
Dad: *Ananda, devru maadthare.*
(God will see to it.)
The next morning, he cycled to the Raghavendra Swami Mutt and put ten rupees in the *hundi.*

· · · · · · · · · · · · · · · · · · ·

(18)

FIGHT NO 540

Of the countless fights that Sriram and I have indulged in, this one sticks out as possibly the most unique. I can't remember the exact number of the fight and that's not even germane to the story. I was in class VII and mom was out of town. She had gone to Madras to attend a family function and was to be back in three days. Dad had his train duty as usual. As was the case, Sriram and I had received our dose of instructions not to squabble in their absence. Being decent folks, they had used the milder term 'squabble' whereas what they were really worried about was one of us maiming the other.

On day two, dad cooked food for us and boarded the 4.30 pm Talguppa Mail. His life was a recurring cycle of the three trains that passed through Shimoga. He was a good cook, and on this day, he had made *bendekayi huli* (bhindi sambar). Sriram and I went out to play in the evening, got home at sunset, did our customary studies and at 9:15 pm, sat down for dinner. Now, a bit of pre-fight background will help you grasp this better. As Kannadigas, our staple food was sambar or rasam with rice, followed by curd rice. Since the beginning, I had the habit of mixing very little curry with my rice. I preferred it less liquidy. In fact, every time we would sit down for a meal, mom always

91

remarked,

Mom: *Swalpa huli haakolo! Adeno shudran tarah thintya!*

(Help yourself to some more sambar. You eat like a shudra!)

This was a telling comment. Without any caste bias, shudras were known to be tightfisted with their curry. Or at least, the brahmins thought so. This probably dates back to centuries when the brahmins had placed themselves at the top of the social hierarchy and were well-to-do. The shudras were at the other end and most of them had to struggle to make ends meet. Therefore, as curry was definitely more expensive than rice, shudras had grown used to having mounds of rice with proportionately lesser curry than the brahmins. I don't know if I was a shudra in my previous birth but I loved eating their way. So much so that extra curry on my rice would kill my appetite. I just couldn't eat like a true-blue brahmin.

Sriram and I settled down at the dining table. It was a modest one-bedroom house with a dining room. To make better use of the space or the lack of it, most houses in the railway quarters had an assortment of things in the dining room. We had a rectangular, metal dining table, mom's sewing machine in a corner, two wooden cupboards and clotheslines above. We sat down with our steel plates that had one-inch rims. I helped myself to rice and Sriram did likewise. The big vessel was half-filled with sambar, clearly way too much for the two of us. I served myself a ladle of sambar and started mixing it with rice. Sriram peered in and saw the quantity still left. He served himself numerous ladles as part of his duty towards wasting nothing. Sriram was 32 years old when he was born, or that's how I felt. That made him almost 47 now and like an old world, over-particular, middle-aged Kannadiga, he believed in all things righteous. Wasting food was a crime that qualified for public flogging. Seeing that I had shirked my duty, he ordered me to finish the rest of it. I brushed him off saying that I preferred to eat like a shudra. The next instant, he upturned the vessel onto my plate. I lost sight of my palm and the rice. The sambar was threatening to overflow from the sides of the plate. In a matter of a few seconds, my dinner, appetite and mental balance were destroyed.

My bile rose and with it my sambar-dipped palm. I swung wildly at him. He was about to feed himself when my palm smashed into his hand. A handful of sambar-rice went flying all over. Before Sriram realized what was going on, I dipped my palm into my plate of food and swung again. Both of us stood up and he was struggling to control the fight. My palm went on dipping itself into my plate of sambar and swinging. I was sobbing and gasping. After the eighth swing, I lost my speed. Sriram had lost his queasiness since he was by now covered in sambar. He held my arm, twisted it behind my back and boned me on my spinal cord with his right elbow. I went flat down howling in pain. He was three years older, three inches taller and maybe 2.3 times stronger. I lay there wincing and after what seemed like a long time, looked up. He was sitting on the chair gathering himself, still trying to come to terms with what had just happened. He barked at me to get up and start cleaning the mess. The damage was quite manic. There were rice and dal flakes all over the room. The walls had splashes and trails of sambar. His t-shirt and shorts were covered in sambar stains. So were mine. A few bhindi pieces were on the sewing machine. He had a curry leaf on the side of his head. The floor was slippery in places. The wooden cupboards also had streaks of dal but they didn't show up as badly as the rest. Some of the clothes drying above carried signs of the rumble. All in all, there was total destruction of the dining room and dinner.

When I could finally focus, I saw him standing with a bucketful of water and a pink mug. He tossed a rag cloth at me. He already had one in his hand. After half an hour of wiping the room clean, we both retired on empty stomachs. The hatred was so heavy that neither of us felt any hunger through the night.

· · · · · · • · • • • • · • · • · · · · ·

(19)

WORLD RECORD

Fifth standard was done and dusted. Summer holidays welcomed us with lazy mornings and active games through the day. The molecules in the air felt lighter as they bounced off our cheeks. The spirit of freedom made us hum songs and fly kites. The only curbs were those that most homes enforced, with varying degrees of leniency. At home, I got up at seven and did whatever I wanted to, mostly reading books or doing an odd sketch. After bath and breakfast, I would step out to play but had to be back home by one. Post lunch, mom and dad always forced me to lie down. They considered it too hot to be out in the afternoons. The only exception was on days when we made kites since this was indoors. We would usually gather at a neighbour's house, make kites out of broadsheets of Deccan Herald or Kannada Prabha, and wait for the evening breeze. The mom of that house would be given prior intimation so that she would boil *sabudana* (sago) for 20-30 minutes, which after cooling down, formed a sticky paste and that was our glue. Evening playtime was from five to seven, give or take fifteen minutes. We had to be back home after dark. After that I usually read a novel, killed a few mosquitoes and generally kept myself occupied till dinner. After dinner, the neighbouring moms usually stood together in the compound and chatted. Some of us also did this till bedtime. This was largely our Summer routine and most families in the railway quarters adhered to it. Being out of the house early in the mornings, in the hot afternoons and after dark was not considered respectable.

On the fourth day of my Summer holidays, I was at home reading a Famous Five novel. It was barely eight in the morning when I heard a knock on the door. It had to be either the newspaper person or the milkman. I was surprised to find Niju standing there, bright and cheerful. Naturally, I thought he had come to the railway station to enquire about some train and had dropped in on his way back. Nijaguna (Niju) was a classmate and a close friend. He lived in an area called Tank Mohalla, which was on the way to school. On most days, our gang stopped at his place en route and cycled together. Tank Mohalla had a large muslim population with a prominent mosque at the beginning of his lane. This area had its own ground rules. Here, one had to really push things before it was considered objectionable. Niju had his huge gang that was made up of both hindus and muslims, most of whom were notorious. They spoke rough, played rough and did pretty wild things. And they didn't have an entry age barrier for this demeanour. Niju's dad was a simple Kannadiga who worked in the postal department. He and his wife had tried their level best to keep Niju out of this gang but had failed miserably. As Niju stepped into my house, my mind searched for the reason he was here so early.

Me: *Stationge bandhidya?*

(Had you come to the station?)

Niju looked around uneasily before asking me.

Niju: *Idee dhina nin jothene irla?*

(Can I be with you the entire day?)

I didn't understand and didn't know what to say.

Me: *Yen aaytho? Gang fighta?*

(What happened? Gang fight?)

He laughed.

Niju: *Ellaru ondhe gangu. Fight henge?*

(Everyone is a part of the same gang. How will we fight?)

I asked him what he was doing away from home so early in the morning. He repeated that he wanted to spend the entire day with me. This created disturbance in my head. My parents would soon start asking difficult questions, on the sly.

1. What is Niju doing here so early?
2. Why hasn't Niju gone home for lunch?
3. Why is Niju at our place in the afternoon?
4. How can his parents allow him to be out the entire day?
5. Has Niju run away or has he been thrown out?
6. Should you be friends with Niju?

I had no answers to any of the above. I looked around uneasily and asked Niju to tell me the real deal.

Niju: *Dabba, kalla police-o!*

(Cops and Robbers!)

I shook my head in utter confusion as he walked in and sat down. Mom gave him a glass of Nutramul and went back into the kitchen while Niju tried to make sense of things for me. What follows is not his words but my explanation of Tank Mohalla's insanity.

Cops and Robbers is a game that's common to almost every child in every part of the world. The cops catch the robbers, and the roles get reversed. This cycle alternates 3-4 times in the course of an hour. This is possible only because the game is played within a small area, one's neighbourhood. This year in Tank Mohalla, someone had changed two small variables, significantly. One was the playing arena. Instead of it being only Tank Mohalla which was logical, it had been extended to include the whole of Shimoga. Now, Shimoga wasn't Bangalore but it wasn't Malgudi either. It was the district headquarters and a sizeable town. If the entire town were to be the playground, the real police force would struggle to nab a gang of robbers, let alone a bunch of boys playing cops. The second rule that had been altered was the active playing time. The game kicked off at eight in the morning and ended at seven in the evening. There were no time-outs. This meant that none of the 12-year-old robbers could have lunch at home else they risked arrest. Once the clock struck seven in the evening, the cops and robbers could get together, and the game resumed at eight the next morning. None of them had even remotely understood the fallout of these two decisions.

On the first day of the Summer holidays, the big Tank Mohalla gang had got together and split into cops and robbers. Taking advantage of the new rule, every robber had run far away from Tank Mohalla. Some robbers had run as far as Sahyadri College, which was on the outskirts.

Some had gone to Mission Compound and a few had hidden beyond the Shimoga bus stand. The entire day had gone by without a single robber being apprehended. Catching anyone without employing a helicopter was a remote possibility. The cops had started off by combing Tank Mohalla. Then they had moved to the neighbouring areas after which they had rushed back to Tank Mohalla, wrongly guessing the robbers would be in their own backyard. After lunch, the cops had headed out again, unsure where to look in the vastness of Shimoga. Then they had given up. At seven in the evening, all the robbers miraculously re-appeared since the active playing time was up. Then both parties got together, played other games and retired for the night. The next morning, they were out of their homes and greeted each other. As the clock inched towards 7:58 am, the robbers ran in different directions.

This moronic game had been going on for three days. Now, on the fourth morning, Niju was at home narrating the proceedings with great glee. I was silent for a few minutes as my mind readjusted itself. I enquired what the cops and robbers did the entire day. He shook his head, a little troubled. Usually, it was fun to be robbers because the cops had to do the hard work of hunting them down. Niju said that their new version had changed the basics in a way no one had expected. The robbers now had a really tough time. They had to be away from home the entire day. Lunch was out of the question. They had to figure out friends' homes in far-flung areas and eat there. Also, in most houses, breakfast wasn't ready before 8:30 and so the robbers left Tank Mohalla without eating. On the other hand, the cops had breakfast, ran around a bit, looked around some more, had lunch at home, slept in the afternoons, ran errands for their moms and led a normal life. The previous day, two cops had reportedly gone for a matinee show as well.
Me: *Niju, ishtondu huchchu thana, life alle kelilla.*
(I haven't heard this kind of stupidity ever in my life.)
He laughed excitedly. I asked him why they didn't stop this moronic game and go back to the normal version.
Niju: *Idhe bombaatu! Ondh dina Shimoga, Thank Mohalla anathe!*
(This madness is nice! Someday, Shimoga will say Thank Mohalla!)

Clearly, skipping breakfast for three days had addled his brain. Mom called me from the kitchen.

Mom: *Niju irthaano, manege hogthaano?*

(Is Niju going to be here or is he going home?)

I mumbled that he would have breakfast with us. Ten minutes later, both of us were gorging on idlis. I got ready quickly and we stepped out.

Me: *Niju, eega plan yenu?*

(What's the plan now?)

Niju checked if he could hang around with me and play whatever games my gang in the railway quarters was planning to play. I nodded but instructed him to not utter a word about their version. We played with my local gang and around noon, I ran home and told mom that Niju was having lunch with us. She arched her right eyebrow considerably. I told her that Niju's grandmother was seriously ill and that his parents had rushed to their village; they would be gone for as long as two weeks. I added that Niju was nervous and had to be around someone; he had chosen me and so for the next several days, he would spend all his waking hours at home. Mom felt terrible and told me to tell Niju that he was welcome to stay with us. I ran out feeling like a champ. I had fixed this and how! After this, the days passed in total bliss. Every morning, Niju landed up at our home at eight. Mom and dad would enquire about his grandmother. Niju would make up logical randomness. We would have breakfast, play, have lunch, sleep, play and he would head back home at 6:45 pm.

Back in Tank Mohalla, every robber had figured out a similar arrangement. The cops stayed back and played other games. They had progressed to playing cricket matches too. Everyone knew what everyone else was up to but they never put a stop to the most stupid game they had invented. Throughout that Summer, the cops stayed cops and the robbers stayed robbers. This was possibly the longest running `Cops and Robbers' game in the history of the world.

· · · · · · · · · · · · · · · · · ·

(20)

BD SPECIAL

I was deep into my third standard homework. It was 7:30 pm and mom was deep into preparing dinner. Dad's train was scheduled to arrive soon. This was the last train into Shimoga. All of a sudden, the railway station siren let out its dreadful wail, three times in succession. This meant only one thing: accident.

I was alarmed but didn't imagine the worst. I closed my books and walked into the kitchen, Sriram right behind me. Mom stood there, covered with panic. She held both of us tightly. It was difficult to say whether she was giving or seeking courage. Fighting back tears, she walked out. Most of the neighbouring women made their way to our house. All the men in the railway quarters were hurrying towards the station. As mom broke down, the women took turns trying to comfort her that nothing terrible would have happened. Sriram and I ran out towards the station. Most of the men on the platform gave us forced smiles and said that nothing bad could have happened. I stood outside the Station Master's cabin. He was frantically dialling numbers and shouting, 'SMET, SMET', the railway code for Shimoga. People were moving in and out of his room, shouting instructions at others to not block the entrance. A few had lit up bidis, chatted in hushed tones and kept shaking their heads confident that nothing bad could have happened. This was just ignorant hope since no one knew anything yet. Sriram and I kept close to the Station Master's room hoping to hear some news. Various men at different points asked us to go home, saying we would be informed the moment there was news. More than an hour passed and no concrete information was forthcoming. I suddenly thought of mom and ran home. Sriram followed soon. Mom had wept herself out by then and was now looking stoic. The women were still there. Mom asked us to have dinner as it was nearly nine. She refused to eat. I wasn't too hungry but mom forced us and we ate quickly. Sriram returned to the station while I stayed back feeling empty. Around 9:45 pm, two railway guards came home. The Station Master had finally received some news: *the train had derailed 40 kilometres from Shimoga. The engine and 3 bogies had slipped off the tracks. There were injuries but no casualties. Dad was safe, the driver and the fireman were fine, rescue work was on, and it would be a long night.*

Mom didn't seem convinced. The guards took turns repeating the same thing. Finally, she looked a bit relieved. Before heading back to the station, they asked the women to head back, have dinner and sleep. The women stayed behind, speaking in unison, each insisting she had always known that nothing bad could have happened. Mom smiled for the first time in hours and kept nodding. Seven minutes later, Sriram ran inside the house and repeated what the guard uncles had said. Mom finally had a small portion of curd rice. Only the next-door aunty was still around. Soon after, I fell asleep in the chair. When I opened my eyes, it was 2 am. Sriram was dozing in the chair next to me but mom was wide awake. She asked us to go in and sleep. Dad came home at 5:30 in the morning. He washed and changed, spoke with mom for a while and fell asleep. It was a Saturday and I had to leave for school at 7:15 am, so mom continued to stay up.

When I got home that afternoon, there was excitement around the railway quarters. Some of the boys told me that they had never seen such a fancy train in their lives, as the one at the station right now. Someone said that it had come all the way from Bangalore. Another added that even Bangalore didn't have such a train, and this one had come all the way from Bombay. The older boys laughed it off saying a train from Bombay could never reach Shimoga overnight. We made our way to the station, talking animatedly. At the first sight of this train, I stopped in my tracks for I hadn't seen anything so beautiful. Shimoga had three sets of tracks, the main one and two shunting tracks. This train sat on the last set, away from the platform. It wasn't the dull brick-red colour that trains usually were but a majestic blue with pink stripes. Just three bogies long, it carried an exotic name: BD SPECIAL. We jumped across the tracks like a herd of goats to inspect it at close range. We ran our fingers over it, climbed the steps to check if any door had been accidently left open, closely checked the wheels and the couplings to see if they were any different from the regular trains and spent a long time discussing its particulars. When we met in the evening, the conversation was again about the BD SPECIAL. Maricruz had gathered information. [*Maricruz lived two houses away and we were thick as thieves. His real name was M Rajesh, and we studied in the same class. His dad, Mangalnathan, was a railway guard (just like dad) and a Tamilian Christian (unlike dad). For some strange reason that even M Rajesh never understood or remembered, one of the nuns in Mary Immaculate had named him Maricruz in LKG. Since then, everyone in school and the railway quarters called him that and it had become his official name. The attendance register and his marks cards carried the same.*]

Maricruz said that Gundu Rao was visiting Shimoga by 'Yelicofter' a week later. He could never say helicopter. Gundu Rao was the Chief Minister of Karnataka. According to Maricruz, the CM was coming into town to inaugurate a polytechnic college. Post that, his family would join him and head to Jog Falls and other places of interest around Shimoga. At the end of their trip, they would return to Bangalore by train and hence BD SPECIAL had already been dispatched. Maricruz was generally erratic with his information but at times, he had also been dead right. The Gundu Rao story made sense. Nobody could understand how he had figured out so much in the past three hours. We looked at Maricruz with awe because he was sharing the Chief Minister's

travel plans with much confidence. Ramu, three years older, was my next-door neighbour and the son of an Asst. Station Master. He and Sriram were of the same age. He sniggered at Maricruz's story.
Ramu: *Hogale! Gundu Rao-oo illa, Mundu Rao-oo illa.*
(What rubbish! No Gundu Rao, no Mundu Rao.)
Ramu asked us if we knew what BD stood for. We looked at him blankly.
Ramu: *BD SPECIAL andre Birthday Specialu!*
(BD SPECIAL means Birthday Special!)
He carried on, in a tone worthy of a scholar.
"It's the 100th birthday of the Wodeyar rulers. If you remember your lessons correctly, the Wodeyar dynasty had been ruling the Mysore State for centuries. Then the British took over but in 1881, power was handed back to them. So, to celebrate this great occasion, they have imported 100 BD SPECIALs from Russia. These 100 trains have been sent to different parts of Karnataka. Starting soon, these trains will crisscross the State giving away biscuits, chocolates and clothes to people along the way."

There was stunned silence. In six sentences, Ramu had given us too much information: local, international, historical and statistical. We stared at him with open mouths big enough to take in the BD SPECIAL itself. He stood there as if he was the Russian Railway Minister himself, the one who had sent these trains to Karnataka. Birthday Special made perfect sense. Slowly, we shook our heads in admiration and praised him for his extraordinary knowledge. Moments later, all of us jumped at the same thought. Biscuits and chocolates! Given the occasion as well as the appearance of the train, we were sure it wouldn't be the usual Parle biscuits and local chocolates. It would most likely be fancy, imported packs. I saw my dad and Giddi's father walking back from the station, ran to them and casually asked dad about BD SPECIAL: did it indeed carry goodies? Dad replied that it was normally stocked with biscuits, chocolates, water, sugar, milk powder, tea and coffee powder, blankets, clothes and other things. I ran back and did a mighty salaam to Ramu.

Over the next couple of hours, the news spread and soon enough, over 80% of the railway quarters' kids knew about the stuff inside. In the space of an evening, theories had got replaced with plots. Our group was quite docile, and we were only wondering how to be in the front line when the distribution finally happened. But elsewhere, some of the older, less restrained groups were planning daring schemes. In the deeper part of the railway quarters which housed most of the class IV employees, some of the groups were quite notorious. One such group was headed by Wiremudi. He was black as coal and strong as a steam engine. He was much older than me and led a band of boys, all potential Wiremudis. We rarely crossed paths with them. Only recently, we had foolishly played our first cricket match against Wiremudi XI. They had won it handsomely but not fairly. Wiremudi was twice LBW, run out once and had yet remained unbeaten on 73.

A couple of days later, we were playing Cops & Robbers, and I had strayed into Wiremudi's area to hide. A boy from his gang, roughly my age, walked up to me. He asked if our gang wanted stuff from BD SPECIAL. They were planning to ransack the train. Sweating with excitement, I waited for the full proposition. He said that for a nominal price, we could have anything they looted.

1 tin of milk powder – Rs.4

1 kilo sugar – Rs.4

2 bars of chocolates – Rs.5

4 packs of biscuits – Rs.4

1 pillow – Rs.6

1 blanket – Rs.10

He then added that we had to pay 50% in advance and the rest on delivery. I meekly said that I would check with the gang and get back to him. I ran back, rounded up the gang and told them about the proposal. There was more alarm than excitement. Everyone felt that this was too daring and risky; not ransacking the train but even buying ransacked goods. I nodded in agreement. We decided to stay away from all this and only try and get our share during distribution. But Wiremudi's deal was too good to let go. I told myself that there had to be a safer way to approach this. That's when I remembered the diary. Since the day mom got married in 1968, she maintained an account of monthly expenses. It was more meticulous than *Chitragupta's* records. I checked the entries and saw that we spent 75 rupees a month on milk. Compared to this, Wiremudi's deal was a steal. It was a chance worth exploring and if I could appeal to mom's economic sense, she might seriously consider it. I would add an extra rupee for every unit and make my 5-6 rupees in the bargain. This was a rare win-win-win arrangement where all three parties would be better off: mom, Wiremudi and me. Of course, there was no way I could mention Wiremudi's gang and the train robbery.

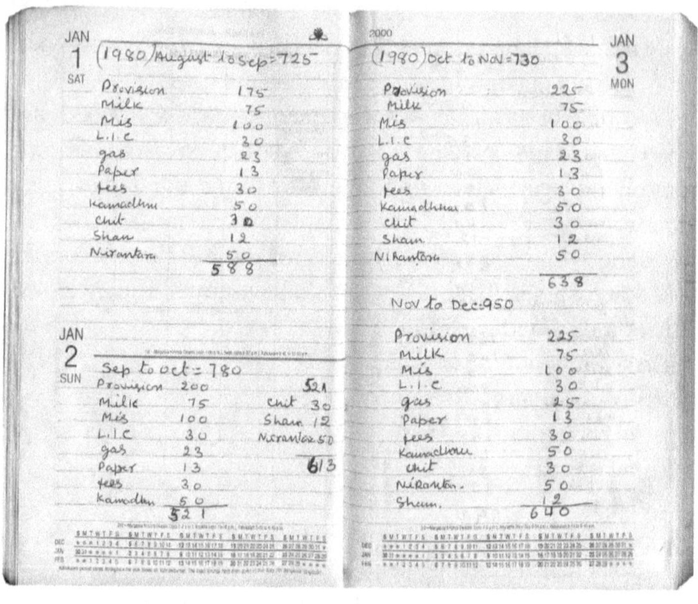

So, I thought up another story. I told mom that one of the petty shop owners where I usually bought peppermint had made me this offer. I spoke in a slightly deeper voice and acted like a grown up. Mom showed interest momentarily but then dismissed it. I insisted and pushed her for an advance. She shook her head and said that it made no sense. `How can anyone get stuff so cheap?', she muttered. In my desperation to convince her and get the deal sealed, I blurted,

Me: *BD SPECIAL, amma!*

At this, Dad lowered the Deccan Herald and asked me what the connection was. Now, my foot was centimetres above a landmine. I needed a few moments to get the story clear in my head. One of my time-buying tactics was to repeat the question loudly and slowly as this gave my mind enough time to spin a story.

Me: *Connectionaaa? Connectionoo heltheeni. Nimige goth idhiyyo ilvo but bhayankara connection idhe.*

(Connection? I'll tell you the connection. I don't know if you are aware of this or not but there's a crazy connection.)

Dad folded the Deccan Herald and looked at me with concern. I started telling him about Gundu Rao, the Wodeyars, 100-year celebrations, Birthday Special, the stuff inside etc. I surmised that maybe the shopkeeper had done a deal with one of the railway employees, was getting stuff from the train at dirt-cheap rates and selling it to us. Dad bunched up his forehead and I could see the pain that he was going through. I quickly added that according to me, this wasn't the right thing to do, but then why bother about their crooked deal as long as we got stuff at cheaper rates?

Dad: *Convent school-ge hogthya but ondh paisa buddhi ilvalla ninge!*

(You go to a convent school but don't have one paisa of intelligence!)

Me (softly): *Huh?*

Dad: *First of all, BD SPECIAL is Breakdown Special.*

He said that BD SPECIAL was in Shimoga because of the derailment and would head back soon. He added that no one could ransack, buy or stealthily bargain with the ease that I had in mind. He also said that if I stopped mixing around with the railway quarters' boys, I would have a better future. He went back to his Deccan Herald. Mom went back to sewing the torn cushion cover. My face turned a dull, brick red. I sat thinking of all the luminaries - Maricruz, Gundu Rao, Ramu, the Russians, the Wodeyars, Wiremudi - and the stinging embarrassment that they had caused me.

. . . .

(21)

GUD BUD

Despite it being a Monday, we were a relaxed lot. Our fifth standard class test had got over the previous week and Pramod was on top of the world. Not that he had done well; far from it. In fact, he was one of those who never stood a fighting chance against any subject. But our class had two kinds of students:
1. Those who celebrated briefly when they scored well.
2. Those who felt like helium balloons whenever tests or exams got over, irrespective of how they had fared.
I don't know whose outlook to life was better. When I enquired, he said that the previous evening, his parents had taken him to have Gud Bud. I had no idea what he was talking about. It sounded like someone had dropped two cardboard boxes.
Me: *Gud Bud?*
He: *Ondhsala taste maadu. Chirthe hinde jinke, ashte!*
(Taste it once. Deer chasing cheetah, that's all!)
`Deer chasing cheetah' was a pet phrase, which meant that the world as we knew stood altered. We didn't use this expression often because anything life-altering wasn't commonplace. Yes, we had used it extravagantly six months earlier when India had won the Benson & Hedges Cup, along with the Audi. And now, Pramod had let it fly. In the days and months that followed, Gud Bud created a frenzy and no one in Shimoga was spared. If we

had our own Time magazine, it would have been the cover story for twelve weeks running. Gud Bud became the Great Divide, splitting the population of Shimoga into Hads and the Not-Yet-Hads.

It was the mother of all ice creams. It came in seven layers and more colours than the most resplendent rainbow. It was served in a glass so tall that the parlour had to import special spoons. We had never seen such long, macho scoopers and these were aptly called 'Bachchan Spoons'. The name Gud Bud was equally exotic. On a casual hearing, it meant 'something amiss'. But if one reflected upon it, the deeper meaning came alive in scoopfuls. The dessert was so big, so heavy and so magical that it created a discontinuity, a-before-and-after in one's ice cream eating experience. Till then, an ice candy was an impulse treat and an ice cream, a planned one. Gud Bud was definitely a planned treat but both 'planned' and 'treat' were in huge multiples. For many families, it took weeks of planning and after the indulgence, the recalled pleasure lasted months. Needless to add, something so out-of-this-world didn't come cheap. For a lot of people in the railway quarters, Gud Bud budget had to be put together. Obviously, this wasn't as big a deal as buying a Sumeet mixie or a National Panasonic 2-in-1. But the cost of each Gud Bud was at least three times more than any other ice cream, and the average family size in the railway quarters was five point three.

We made the trip nearly two months after the Gud Bud storm had begun raging. We were late to the Gud Bud experience and a lot of people I knew had crossed over by then. This wasn't ideal for my emotional state but I had made peace with it. Since a very young age, I had been blessed with equanimity in the face of tough circumstances. Each family had its own positives and negatives and one had to learn to live with them, happily. For instance, I wasn't just the first, but also the only one in school to have driven a train. Even people who lived in houses the size of the Shimoga railway station could never dream of doing this. So, I'd won some, lost some. Finally, a Sunday was chosen. This was decided on Saturday itself because this decision had implications. First of all, Sriram and I had to sacrifice our evening games since we had to leave home by 5:30 pm. Panchatara Ice Cream Parlour stood at the beginning of Nehru Road, and was a good twenty-five minutes' walk. There we would have to wait our turn. On a Sunday evening, people sometimes queued for close to an hour. So, on Saturday itself, I broke the news about my unavailability the next evening. My cricket team captain had twenty-four hours to re-think the pace attack and re-draw his strategies. The other crucial thing to be decided was food. Mom had to measure the quantity of Sunday lunch so that there would be no leftovers. After the Gud Bud feast, we wouldn't have the stomach for dinner.

Sunday evening arrived and I was ready ahead of time. At 5:15 pm, mom was still combing her hair. Dad had stepped out on some errand and was to be back any minute. God picked this precise moment to send one of our neighbours to borrow something from our kitchen and this led to frivolous, aimless banter between mom and her. I made faces of impatience at mom but she continued chatting irresponsibly. Finally, at 6:25 pm, almost an hour later than the time we had originally planned, I led them to Panchatara. When we arrived at the parlour, a big queue had already formed outside. They had a man specially to tell customers how long each group had to wait. It was a thankless job. When people exclaimed, `45 *minutes!*', he looked at them without expression, waiting for them to decide if they wanted to stay or turn back and risk being called idiots by strangers, friends and family members. Dad had to wait for three minutes before he could enquire how long our wait would be. We were given a time of about thirty minutes. While dad spoke to the `waiting time' man, I quickly calculated. There were twenty-three people in the queue including us. In the two minutes that dad had been speaking to him, two more families totalling seven people had arrived. I looked at some of the people who were present before us and felt angry. Then I saw the later ones and felt sorry. I was being stupid.

The parlour was a part of a small shopping complex situated one level lower than the road. It had a glass front that carried the menu painted in red. Apart from the usual range of juices (mosambi, orange, grape, watermelon, ganga jamuna etc.), and the standard ice creams (vanilla, chocolate, strawberry etc.), the parlour also had, a craze from a few years earlier: cassatta. That had caused traffic jams but not a social divide like the Gud Bud. I looked through the glass frontage and saw a waiter carrying a tray with four Gud Buds. I fleetingly took in the layers and the colours. The Gud Bud glass was massive. It had a narrow bottom that widened as it rose.

Me: *Amma, ulta Qutub Minar thara idhe but Qutub Minar kintha baala sakkat aagide.*

(Mom, it's like an inverted Qutub Minar, only more glorious.)

Since mom was from Delhi and my grandparents still lived there, we used to visit them every Summer for a couple of weeks. I had seen all the monuments in Delhi. During our history class, I had extra information about Allauddin Khilji and Qutubuddin Aibak, and had described the size and grandeur of Delhi to the class. I had even climbed up to the first floor of Qutub Minar. I had been lucky. A couple of years after my visit, there was a stampede of school children; many died tragically and going up Qutub Minar was stopped forever.

Me: *Qutub Minaru ondhe colouru but Gud Bud ondh ondh levelu ondh ondh colouru.*

(Qutub Minar is just one colour but Gud Bud has one one colour for one one level.)

Mom's mind was elsewhere and she didn't answer. I went back to the menu painted on the glass front. Gud Bud had been placed in chronological order. It was the last thing on the menu and surprisingly, painted in the same size as the rest of the items. This seemed odd. Atma was the best student in the seventh standard and naturally the school leader. He had a special badge signifying his status. By the same token, I had expected Gud Bud to be painted much bigger or at least placed right on top. But going by the menu, it was a last bencher. There was no hint on the menu as to where it stood in its class. Since we had to wait for a while, I asked mom about this. She didn't have a ready answer. She usually thought deeply about sarees and not ice creams. After looking vacant for a minute, she surprised me with an answer that made sense. She remarked that this was the only place in Shimoga that sold Gud Bud and hence there was no need to even put its name down.

I kept staring through the glass front to see which tables were close to finishing. There were a lot of small kids inside and the Gud Bud glass was really tall. Most of them couldn't take a spoonful without either spilling or toppling the glass over. So, every parent was helping his or her child. The parents themselves had their own Gud Buds to finish. On top of this, every person would have a spoonful and then talk animatedly. At this rate, no one looked likely to finish for at least two hours more. I went to the man at the entrance and asked him to tell the people inside to hurry. I also reminded him that we were numbers 19-23. He nodded without much enthusiasm. It was nearly 6:57 pm and the skies were turning dark. A family of five finally walked out and numbers 1-4 went in. Ten minutes later, 5-8 got their table. Mom took out her irritation on me saying that by shuffling restlessly and staring through the glass, the people inside wouldn't gobble up their ice creams. I muttered that the ones inside shouldn't be allowed to talk. They could always sing its praises once they got out. I wanted dad to step up and get us going. He was nowhere in sight.

Me: *Amma! Where is appa?*

(Mom, where is dad?)

She said that she had sent him across the road to buy a gasket. I stared at her in disbelief. Their perspectives and priorities were appalling. Were they becoming senile? As soon as he returned, I told him in exasperation,

Me: *Appa, goods train kintha slow aage hogtha ide.*

(Dad, this is moving slower than a goods train.)

Dad: *Irli. Life alli swalpa patience irbeku.*

(It's okay. We have to have some patience in life.)

Most of dad's remarks were at a life level, rarely at the situation-at-hand level. With a sharp glance at mom, I said with bitterness that we should have left home at our appointed time. There was a sudden movement as numbers 9-13 rushed inside, as if they were late for an appointment with God. Then, another table cleared and 14-18 broke into frenzied action. We were surely about ten minutes away from our out-of-body experience. I excitedly told mom to tell her stomach to make way for Qutub Minar. Mom and dad paid little attention and looked past me at the parlour door. The previous group was still at the entrance having a discussion with the `waiting man', who was telling them something and shaking his head. I thought he was telling the group that they wouldn't be allowed more than ten minutes to finish their Gud Bud, as I'd suggested. Dad walked up and joined the group. After three intense minutes of conversation, the two kids in that group began to wail. I sensed that something was terribly wrong. The parents kissed their two howling kids and walked away as dad walked back to us. I was so tense that my tongue was paralysed.

Mum: *Yen anthe?*

(What is it?)

Dad looked uncomfortable.

Dad: *Swalpa thondre aagogide.*

(There's a slight problem.)

The parlour had run out of ingredients for one layer. We could either have 6 layers or come back the next day. I was devastated and angry and tearful and suicidal. My own 4-layered Gud Bud had formed inside. Dad looked at me with his every-issue-has-to-be-handled-with-composure look. I looked back at him, looking nothing like his son.

Dad: *It's okay. Ondh nimisha. Yochne maadona.*

(It's okay. One minute. Let's think.)

If only we had left at the appointed hour! I glowered at mom. I had waited two months and one part of me desperately wanted to go in and have it, the 6/7th Gud Bud. Mom, Dad and Sriram were also not happy with the situation but they were indifferent. We had planned for so long, waited for so long that it was better to be done with it. But the final call was mine.

Mom: *Anand, bega decide maadu.*

(Decide quickly.)

In every Gud Bud conversation I had been a part of, every layer was discussed in great detail. Each layer evoked delight of a different kind and being one short didn't equal to having Gud Bud. Also, the next day in school, I would reach a point in my conversation where I would get called out badly. I could always ask the 'waiting man' about the missing layer and get its ingredients and description. But at the end of the day, I would have to live with the lie and that would kill me. I said the three most difficult words, in my thinnest voice,

Me: *Next week barona.*

(We'll come back next week.)

Mom twined her forefinger around the edge of her sari.

Mom: *Aa ondh layer bidu. Adhe vanilla athva strawberry irathe…swalpa dry fruits haakirthaane, ashte!*

(Forget that one layer. It'll be the usual…vanilla or strawberry… possibly with some dry fruits, that's all!)

Me: *Jog Falls-ge hogi Roarer nod dhe bartheera?*

(Will you go to Jog Falls and come back without seeing Roarer?)

Jog Falls was tourist magnet and a regular picnic destination for most people in Shimoga. It fell in four magnificent streams and these were aptly named:

Raja. For its majestic flow.

Rani. For its grace.

Roarer. For its thundering sound.

Rocket. For its speed.

Tourists timed their visit, and during monsoon, people checked the amount of rainfall and the mist levels before heading there. Sometimes, they were unlucky because one or two streams would not be in full force or visible. If one didn't see all four streams in all their glory, one could never claim that he or she had seen Jog. Mom could not argue with this logic. We turned around. To make up for this misfortune and the lack of dinner at home, we went to Vaishali Hotel and had butter masala dosa.

Seven days later, I finally sat down with the seven layers of Gud Bud.

· · · · · · **· · · · ·** · · · · · ·

(22)

JUNE-JULY

It was an inconspicuous Sunday afternoon, and I was at home along with Sriram. Dad was on duty and mom had gone to Mohan's shop. Mohan was a pioneer in Shimoga, in the tape-recording business. Armed with a National Panasonic 2-in-1, he made compilations of songs on TDK cassettes and earned a lot of money. He usually took a week for each assignment. This was one of the few things that mom indulged in. She regularly made lists of Hindi songs (Kishore Kumar, Mohammed Rafi, Mukesh, Lata Mangeshkar, Manna Dey etc.) and every few months, added a cassette or two, to her collection.

Sriram was reading a magazine while I was immersed in a novel. I put the book down, possessed with a sudden urge to eat jaggery and tamarind. I traipsed to the kitchen and was helping myself when that irritating voice said from behind,

Sriram: *Oye! Waste maadbeda. Baatlige haaku.*

(Don't waste it! Put it back in the bottle.)

My glare could have burnt the skin off anyone else, but he didn't even flinch. Grabbing the bottle from my hand, he put it back on the shelf and ordered me out of the kitchen. My bile rose. About eight months earlier, we had had Fight No.540. We had continued to fight over silly issues but they hadn't been remarkable; a few curses, a slap here and there, some pushing around, threats of informing mom and dad about my choice of foul words etc. This time I decided against physical assault. I had learnt my lesson the hard way. Instead, I chose psychological torture. I muttered that if eating a piece of jaggery was wastage, I would show him the real meaning of it. I strode out of the kitchen. Sriram saw my *Ravana-avatar* and followed me wondering what was going through my ten heads. I went to the backyard and clambered up June-July. We had two guava trees, side by side. Eight feet up, where they branched out, the two had grown into each other. Since they looked like inseparable twins to me, I had named them June-July.

We didn't have them a few years ago. One day, dad had brought home some delicious guavas of both varieties, white and red. The red guavas were not as widely available as the white ones. While both were equally tasty, the red guavas looked more alluring when sliced. Both sets had big seeds. Mom always instructed us to spit out the seeds or risk getting a stomachache. I wasn't very comfortable with them as they regularly got stuck between my teeth. Sriram and I stood in our little backyard, feasting on a guava each. He had chosen white, and I had picked red. We kept spitting out the seeds on the little bed of soil. A week later, we noticed two small saplings. At this point, we didn't realize that the seeds we spat out had given birth to two guava trees. Within three months, they had become big enough to go to school. I started taking care of them and within the next two years, they turned into tall trees. Pretty soon, they started flowering and suddenly one day, they bore fruit in abundance. I cannot describe the excitement at home.

I wanted to be the first to taste them. Mom held me back saying that I should at least wait for the guavas to start ripening. With great difficulty, I restrained myself for two days. That weekend, I ran up the tree. Mom and Sriram looked up with much eagerness. I plucked one and bit into the best guava I had tasted all my life. It was difficult to say which tree it belonged to as the branches interleaved into each other. Mom asked me to throw down a few and Sriram didn't miss a single catch. I told mom that I would stay up on the tree and eat twenty-five guavas.

Mom: *Kelega ba. Aaram aage thinnu. Kothi tarah thin beda.*

(Come down. Eat in comfort. Don't eat like a monkey.)

Just before coming down, I decided to have one more. I randomly plucked another and bit into it.

Me: *Ammmmaaaaa!*

She looked up in alarm. I held out the bitten fruit to her. It was red inside. Either June was white, and July was red, or the other way around. God had chosen us. That day onwards, we became the house of plenty.

Every day, I would eat half a dozen guavas. We regularly distributed some to our neighbours. At will, I would dole them out to my friends. As the season progressed, the guavas started challenging us. June-July bore so many fruits that we had a new batch of *Kauravas* each day. It was abnormal. In the evenings, mom and I would look up and count a few that we felt would ripen over the subsequent 2-3 days. But the next morning, there would be several dozen perfectly ripe guavas. I was the principal harvester, and it became a part of my morning duty. During the peak season that lasted about a month and a half, June-July showered us with 4-5 dozen guavas every day without fail. The house carried an overwhelming smell of guavas even after mom bathed and generously applied Ponds talcum powder. We started distributing them to more families in the quarters and yet, we would be left with more. Mom hit upon an idea and turned them into jam. Idlis, dosas, chapatis, bread etc. were now served with guava jam. Then, we started distributing jam to our near and dear ones. Such was their fertility that every season, we would have plenty of weeks of plenty.

Back to our fight, I perched myself on one of the branches. Sriram was looking up wondering what I was about to do next. He vaguely suspected that I was going to hit him with guavas and hence looked a bit shifty. But I had decided against assault.

Instead, I plucked a guava, took a small bite, held up the rest of it to him and threw it over our compound wall. I was bent on showing him what wastage really meant. Within two minutes, I had done the same thing with fifteen guavas. I was enjoying my sweet revenge, in both white and red colours. Sriram looked visibly shaken. His face screamed murder, of two kinds: what I was doing with the guavas and what he wished to do with me. The guavas were strewn on the ground outside the compound wall. A handsome family of pigs came scavenging and started enjoying the fruit. I yelled out to Sriram,

Me: *Nodu! Waste maadthilla. Paapa handhi-ge thinstha idheeni.*

(Look! I am not wasting them. I am feeding the poor pigs.)

It was difficult to say who was angrier. He strode back into the house. But I wasn't done. That day, I cleaned out June-July. Every guava (including those in their early teens and childhood) was fed to the pigs. It was only six days later that I again started harvesting guavas by the dozen.

· · · · · ● · ● ● ● · ● · · · ·

(23)

A SCENE FROM A MOVIE

It was half past five on a glorious evening. The sun smiled warmly on our neighbourhood. I was back from school and sitting on top of the mango tree diagonally across the house. A bunch of us were playing *mara kothi,* an arboreal, athletic game. *Mara kothi* literally means `tree monkey'. The loser draws a circle in the ground under the tree, places a stick inside it and counts to twenty-five. The others scamper up and take their positions on various branches. The loser has to then clamber up and touch someone to make him the loser. While he makes his move up the tree, if anyone swings down from a branch and touches the stick, the loser has to start again. The risk-averse sit pretty on the higher branches. The adventurous ones balance themselves precariously at the edge of the lower branches so that they can swing down quickly. I was fairly high up on the tree when I saw one of the railway peons entering our house. This was a little troubling since no official messenger came home unless it was terribly important. Dad was on train duty and was slated to arrive home at 7:10 pm. As my focus shifted between the house and the stick, mom yelled my name in a high-pitched voice. The first thing that occurred to me was that there had been an accident. I yelled back, swung down from the branch and ran into the house.

Mom looked visibly shaken. She thrust a twenty-rupee note

into my palm, along with a list (a kilo of sugar, half a kilo of copra, 100 gm cashews, 50 gm raisins) and asked me to fetch the items in double-quick time. I didn't understand what was going on. I scooted out and was back in 15 minutes. Giddi's mom had come over and was grating coconut. The pressure cooker was already whistling, milk was being boiled while mom was chopping potatoes into fine pieces. Between efforts to catch my breath, I asked her what was going on. Attending to many vessels at the same time, she said that dad's train was at Birur and that he had sent an urgent message to prepare a feast by the time the train pulled into Shimoga. She added that she was racing against time, and hadn't expected a thing like this in her wildest dreams, and that's why she had requested Anasuya (Giddi's mom) to help her out, and that she was so lucky to have a friend like her, and that hopefully all the dishes tasted fine despite this haste, and that they would like her preparation. Her sentence was longer than the longest train that passed through Shimoga.

Me: *Yen helthidheera? Nanige ondh paisa artha aagilla!*

(What are you saying? I haven't understood a paisa.)

Mom: *Yaaro cinema director-ge oota thogondu hogbek anthe.*

(We are supposed to take food for some cinema director.)

I was even more confused. But it didn't matter to mom. In fact, I didn't matter to her at all as she went back to orchestrating her eight vessels and five dishes, all at various stages of preparation. She was squishing tamarind, frying groundnuts, grating carrots, peeling peas, squeezing a lemon, telling her friend Anasuya what to do next and in the midst of all this, suddenly turned to me and asked me to go next door and borrow their large tiffin carrier. I did as I was told. With her back to me, mom instructed me again to take out our tiffin carriers, wash them thoroughly and wipe them dry. Like a zombie errand boy, I did that too. Through all this, Sriram was trying to concentrate on his studies but he too looked kind of unfocussed, more than he usually did. Again, without looking at me, mom asked me to open the small Godrej and pull out a couple of fresh napkins. The genie in me did that in two minutes. The next task was to take out two large plastic *buttis* (interwoven bags) and make sure that they didn't have a speck of dirt on them.

I was excited without knowing why, but also tired and irritated. I went to the drawing room and sat under the fan. Mom called out asking me for the exact time. It was 6:35 pm. The feast was ready soon after. Giddi's mom started packing the tiffin carriers.

Mom rushed to the bathroom, washed and changed into her best sari and looking unnecessarily self-conscious, came and sat under the fan. Giddi's mom placed the tiffin carriers and little steel boxes in the buttis and finally came and sat under the fan as well. For the third and the final time, I asked her for an explanation, one I would understand.

Mom: *Aa peonu yeno ardham bardha heldha. Nanagu full kathe gothilla.*

(That peon said something half-baked. Even I don't know the full story.)

She adjusted her sari and continued,

Mom: *Appana yaaro doddu director friendu, Puttanna Kanagal bartha idhaare.*

(Dad is coming with a big director friend of his, Puttanna Kanagal.)

She checked with Giddi's mom if the talcum powder was showing in places.

Mom: *Station-ge oota thogondu banni antha appa message kalsidhru.*

(Dad had sent message that we should carry food to the station.)

Mom again checked with her friend if the sari was fine and then hurried both Sriram and me to change into our best clothes and look presentable.

A little over two hours ago, dad's train was at Birur. After completing all his procedures, he climbed into the Guard's compartment and leaned out with the green flag as it was still daylight. Closer to Shimoga, the flag would be folded, and the lantern would come out. The whistle was in his hand, ready to be blown. As he leaned out and was about to wave the flag, he noticed a huge crowd outside the first-class compartment, somewhere in the middle of the train. The throng was shouting and jostling. He also noticed a couple of Railway Police constables in the crowd and realized that something was wrong.

In all likelihood, a thief had been spotted and he had locked himself inside the compartment. From a distance, he could also see the driver leaning out and looking towards him for the green signal. Dad sighed and with the flag in hand, walked down to the crowd. He asked what the matter was and instructed them to clear out as it was time for the train to depart. An over-excited section of the crowd responded,

Crowd: *Aydh nimsha, saar. Ondhu autograph beku, saar.*

(Five minutes, sir. Just need an autograph, sir.)

Dad pulled aside one of the guys and asked who was travelling in the train. He was told that the famed Kannada director Puttanna Kanagal Sir, was inside. Dad had no idea who this person was. He was so caught up with his day-to-day life that he never watched movies. His count stood at a measly dozen films since birth. He shrugged, more concerned about getting the train going. He noticed that the director had closed his compartment door. After unsuccessfully trying to disperse the crowd, he realized that the best option was to request him to step out for a couple of minutes and wave at the people gathered. He climbed into the bogie, knocked on the compartment and said that he was the Guard. Puttanna Kanagal Sir slid open the door and treated dad with great courtesy. He turned out to be a very simple man, just like dad. Dad apologized profusely and requested him to wave at the crowd. Puttanna Kanagal Sir obliged and waved at the cheering crowd which turned cheerful instantly. As dad watched the proceedings, a distant memory told him that he knew this man. With an unsure voice,

Dad: *Saar, sorry, dayavittu bejaar maadko bedi but neevu Mysore alli schooling maadidhra?*

(Sir, sorry, please don't mind but did you do your schooling in Mysore?)

The director nodded and looked at dad with mild interest.

Dad: *Saar, sorry, but Banumaiah's alli idhra?*

(Sir, sorry, but were you at Banumaiah's?)

[Banumaiah was a very wealthy merchant in the state of Mysore. His was a rags-to-riches story. In his early days, he had no money to study.

When destiny gave him the kind of money that he hadn't ever imagined, he spent large sums on setting up schools and colleges. Over decades, the Banumaiah Trust set up some of the most reputed educational institutes in Mysore.]

The director nodded again and looked at dad with more curiosity.

Dad: *Saar, sorry, but naavu ondhe class alli odhidhu ansathe.*

(Sir, sorry, but I feel we studied in the same class.)

The director looked at dad as closely as he would watch his actors.

Puttanna Kanagal: *Subbu?*

Subbu was dad's name. These two had been classmates in the third standard. Both were now in their early 50s; one a celebrated director, the other a railway guard and in two minutes, after decades, they had recognized each other. Whoever had said this knew something deeper about life: history repeats itself, only the names change. This was playing out like a sequel to Krishna & Sudama.

[Like Banumaiah, Puttanna Kanagal hailed from a poor family and went through hard times. He had worked as a cleaner, salesman, teacher and driver to make ends meet. Now, he was a critically acclaimed director with films in Kannada, Telugu and Tamil. He also directed a Hindi movie, `Zehreela Insaan' and the song `Oh hansini' easily stood out as one of the most beautiful and popular numbers. He was credited with giving breaks to several actors and actresses.]

Dad: *Yenu thondre illa andre Shimoga dhalli oota mane indha thurs bidtheeni.*

(If it's not an issue, I'll have dinner arranged from home at Shimoga.)

Puttanna Kanagal politely asked him not to undertake this trouble.

Dad: *Thondre illa...baala khushi, sammana...dayavittu?*

(No problem at all...much happiness, honour...please?)

Dad quickly got off the bogie and looked to his right. The driver was looking in his direction wondering about the cause of the delay. Dad gestured to him that everything was under control. He dashed to the Station Master's cabin and placed an urgent call to Shimoga station. Ten minutes later, the peon had reached home.

The three of us were ready along with the three buttis. Giddi's mom took leave. Mom looked tense and checked her sari for the fourteenth time.

Me: *Appana friendu nimigenu picture alli thogollala. Relax, amma.*
(Dad's friend will not cast you in his movie. Relax, mom.)
I always cracked jokes with mom, never with dad. Though the station was three minutes away, it would take us close to ten minutes today. We would have to walk gingerly so that food wouldn't spill. I felt it was time to leave but mom insisted that we wait for the station bell. Outside the Station Master's cabin was a 4-foot piece of railway track suspended from a beam above. Towards the bottom was a small hole that held an iron rod, about a foot in length. Every time, a train coming into Shimoga reached the outskirts, the peon took the small iron rod and struck the longer one. This could be heard at home. Mom said that we should time our departure to the bell and not earlier. She was worried that dad's colleagues on the platform would get nosey. Three minutes later, we locked the house and walked delicately towards the station. As the train pulled in, mom checked her sari once more. Dad came running and we entered the first-class compartment. The three of us were introduced to Puttanna Kanagal. Mom put her hands together and did a namaste. He pinched my cheeks and enquired after my favourite subjects. I said Biology and Bruce Lee and started getting into details. Dad and mom butted in saying he should eat quickly as the train would depart in 20 minutes. The train would carry onward to Talguppa, the last stop on this leg. The tracks ended there. A short drive away was Sagara Town, blessed with the magnificent Jog Falls. This region was lush green with hills, rivers, waterfalls and naturally, many scenic spots. Puttanna Kanagal was headed there to shoot the movie, *Amrutha Galige.*
Mom spread out the tiffin boxes. He helped himself to two chapatis, some *palya* (sabzi), lemon rice and a bowl of kheer, and

complimented mom on her cooking.

Mom: *Jaldi nalli maadidhu. Ruchi hengidhyo gothilla. Normally, idikintha chennage irathe.*

(This was done in great haste. Not sure of the taste. Normally, it's better than this.)

I cringed. Even if mom had been informed of the visit three months earlier, she would have said the same thing. I had heard a lot of women say similar things. Either they always cooked in haste or never managed their best. After he was done, I took the crockery to the toilet to rinse them. A small group of people outside asked me to get autographs and I acted as if I didn't hear them. It was five minutes to departure and Puttanna Kanagal invited us to attend the shoot over the weekend. We heard the whistle, said goodnight and hurried off the train. Some of the railway employees asked dad with great curiosity how he knew Puttanna Kanagal so intimately.

Dad: *Devaru mahime.*

(Lord's benediction.)

When asked why he had hidden this piece of news from them all these years, dad wasn't sure how to explain and merely shrugged his shoulders. On our way home, he told us in detail about his chance encounter. Needless to add, this was relayed to countless people the next day by mom, Sriram and me. That night, we were four and there was food for fourteen. As talk continued about movies and movie stars over dinner, I remarked deliberately,

Me: *Amma, palya dhalli swalpa uppu jaasthi, chitranna ke innondhu swalpa nimbe rasa bekithu.*

(Mom, sabzi is a little salty and the lemon rice could have had a little more lime.)

Mom muttered that she knew she had messed up something. After dinner, mom and dad made plans to go for the shoot over the weekend. Sriram and I weren't a part of this as we had our class tests the following week.

They left for Sagara on Saturday morning and came back the following night. This was the first film shoot anyone in our family had ever attended. Mom told us many details but the recurring point was that she hadn't seen anything so boring in her life.

There was one scene with five lines of dialogues, and they re-did the same over two days. Mom added that I should have attended the shoot; I would then never complain about pujas being the most boring rituals on earth. I found this hard to believe even though dad echoed her sentiments. But then, he found the conversations at Nayyar's Tailoring Shop more entertaining than Sholay. The unit was travelling back three days later by Bangalore Mail. Their train from Talguppa would come into Shimoga and after a 40-minute stop, leave for Bangalore at 9:50 pm. This time, it wasn't just the director but also the stars: Ramakrishna, Sridhar and Padma Vasanthi. Mom and dad had informed them that we would make their dinner arrangements.

On Wednesday, Giddi's mom came home and both women went berserk again. The spread consisted of chapatis, two kinds of *palya* (sabzi), *chitranna* (lemon rice), *puliyogare* (tamarind rice), carrot *kosambri* (salad), vadas, *sandige* (sabudana papads) and *shavige payasa* (semolina payasa). I knew my drill with the tiffin carriers and the *buttis*. This time, the big difference was the crowd. Firstly, there were stars present and secondly, word had spread. The railway platform resembled a *jaatre* (fair). There were people stuck to the bogie and the RPF men were trying their best to control the mob. Upon seeing us, the crowd parted and we walked through like divine beings. Over their sumptuous dinner, they chatted with us with much interest and enthusiasm. All four were sweeter than mom's *payasa*. Many people in the crowd kept shouting my name, asking me to get them autographs. It seemed inappropriate to me, and I ended up making a few enemies that night. As the train was about to leave, Puttanna Kanagal told dad and mom that when they visited Bangalore, they should drop in, meet his wife and children and have lunch with them. As the train began to move, we thanked them and got off. On our way home, I distinctly heard a few people curse me.

Three months later, we were in Bangalore for a few days to attend a family function. Mom and dad weren't sure if he had honestly meant his invitation. In their minds, it was a discomforting situation and they weren't particularly keen. After some deliberation, dad told mom that it behooved them to ring up Puttana Kanagal since he had said so. They decided to do the perfunctory call. They rehearsed a few lines and excuses depending on how the conversation might play out. Honestly, they hoped that their call would go unanswered. Dad fished out the scrap of paper on which he had scribbled his phone number. The three of us stood around as he dialled the number. A few seconds later,

Dad: *Hello! Hello! Puttana? Naanu Subbu. Heng idheera, saar? Neevu busy irbeku! Bengaluru-ge bandhidheevi...family function-ge. Naavu swalpa busy-ne. Devru volledh maadli. Nimma Mrs-ge namma namaskara helbidi. Next time-oo phone maadtheeni.*

(Hello! Hello! Puttana? This is Subbu. How are you, sir? You must be busy! We are in Bangalore...for a family function. We are also somewhat busy. God bless you. Convey our wishes to your missus. We will call you next time.)

The three of us smiled with relief. Dad had delivered his lines perfectly with the assurance of a seasoned actor. After a pause,

Dad: *Lunch-a?*

We were nonplussed. The director had stressed that he would be unhappy if we didn't pay him a visit and furthermore insisted that we have lunch with his family. Despite this, it was a tentative visit and so, dad and mom decided it was best that just the two of them went. Sriram and I were happy to stay back and catch up with our cousins. For once, the roles got reversed. We hurried them into getting ready since they had to change two buses to get there. Mom and dad got back in the evening after spending a few hours. They met his wife Lakshmi, had lunch and chatted like good old friends.

A strange bond of simplicity and nostalgia developed between the two couples and they stayed in touch. A couple of years later, the guard informed me that the director passed away unexpectedly. Mom and dad continued to meet his wife

* * * * * * * * * * * * * * * * *

(24)

GLASS BOWLS

The annual Social Day was two weeks away and our evenings were filled with rehearsals: recitation, drama, singing (solo and group), mono acting and group dance. Social Day was high-stakes; each class would be pitted against the other, the points across various events added and one eventual winner declared. For the thirteenth time in rehearsal, we crooned our handpicked Kannada folksy song. The chosen singers, eight girls and six boys belonged to class VII A. Our section had to win it against VII B, else we would leave the last year at MIHPS with our heads down in shame. I was good at a few things and usually earned valuable points for my section. I did mono acting, was good at recitation and took part in plays. But my singing was an embarrassment. Certain privileges came with my position as school leader and so I had been inducted into this as well. I was also a part of the athletics and kabbadi teams. I wasn't the best in these but wasn't a total loser either. I could hold my own. Each section got its own teacher as the Social Day in-charge, and we had been assigned the best, Yvonne Miss. For obvious reasons, we called her Even Miss. A name starting with `Y' and followed by `v' was a bit much for Shimoga. She taught us maths, was big built and had a pushy personality. With her, we had an advantage. But an even bigger plus, as we were soon to discover, was Saleemuddin Khwaja. He was a big, lazy boy who wrote very slowly and wasn't particularly bright. When we finished our final rehearsal for the day and trooped out, we passed Even Miss at the door. She gave us an enigmatic, one of those `I know something you don't' smiles. I saw Saleem standing behind her.

The next evening, we took our positions in front of the empty classroom while Even Miss leaned against one of the benches. As usual, we were about to begin our rehearsals when she grinned widely.

Even Miss: *I have great news. This year, we have a few good singers and I am sure we will win. But let me just say that in the history of MIHPS, what we are about to do has never been done. Saleem!*

He walked in with a tabla. All of us were gobsmacked. Saleem had been our classmate for years and yet none of us knew that he played the tabla. The situation looked extremely strange. Probably, Even Miss had thought of a visual drama to impress the judges and the audience. With an encouraging nod from her, Saleem sat down with his tabla and let his fingers fly. The room hushed. After a few minutes, he looked up at all of us and beamed. Then, Even Miss beamed followed by the rest of us. We, Section VII A, felt invincible. The rehearsals took longer as we kept watching Saleem and forgetting our lines. Gradually, we fell into a nice rhythm and there wasn't the faintest doubt who would ace the contest in 1984. When we were done, Even Miss asked Saleem to hide the tabla in the Staff Room. She then told us that no one in school should get a whiff of this; it would be our secret till the big day. We clapped as Saleem picked up the tabla set and walked out of class. As I cycled home, my mind was restless. Something was stirring inside. Three more days of rehearsals went by and the weekend arrived.

On Saturday afternoons, mom and I usually spent an hour in front of the television. From time to time, Doordarshan coughed up something interesting. On this day, it was a cultural programme. A person I couldn't recognize played shehnai, which I found utterly boring. But the presenter praised him excessively and then announced that the next artiste was an `anootha' musician. I asked mom what it meant. She hmmm-ed and said `abnormal' before correcting herself to `rare'. The `anootha' man, clad in a kurta pyjama, smiled at the presenter and took the stage.

Mom and I looked at each other in amusement. He sat down behind a line of glass bowls.

Me: *Amma, ivanu oota swalpa late aagi maadtha idhane.*

(Mom, he's having a late lunch.)

She laughed. The musician did a namaste and said that he was playing an instrument called *jaltarangam*. The camera panned across his glass bowls, which were filled with water to different levels. He held up a stick in each hand and started hitting the rims. *Ting Tung Ting Tung.* Each bowl made a slightly different *Ting Tung* sound depending on the amount of water it held. The instrument looked beguiling. I had no knowledge of music but whatever he played sounded quite arbitrary. After five minutes of this, mom was bored and got up to switch off the television. I yelled, `NO!'. My mind was cooking. This hitherto unknown, unseen, unheard-of and unheard instrument was a godsend. It was simple to make, practice and play. My mind raced ahead to the Competition Day. If some people in the audience withstood the wonder of the tabla and didn't swoon, the *jaltarangam* would surely take care of them. Our act would go down in the annals of MIHPS. I sat through the entire hour of this repetitive performance just in case he brought up any new things or tricks. Nothing new came up, so I switched off the television and went to the showcase.

It wasn't really a showcase but mom called it one. It was a groove in the wall about two feet deep with a couple of cement shelves that was covered with a homemade curtain. For years, it had held a few plastic and glass bowls that were taken out only when special guests visited. We had two sets of glass bowls, five of each. I carefully took out seven, one entire set and two from the other. I had elementary knowledge of music – *Sa Re Ga Ma Pa Da Ni Sa* – though I was shaky about their purpose and the correct way to employ them. But it was as clear as glass that the last note was a repeat of the first, and this meant that I had to hit the first bowl again. I placed the seven notes in the backyard and filled them with water. Visibly, each note got a different amount. I picked up the broom and started looking for the healthiest sticks when my palm smote my forehead. Mom was an ardent sweater-knitter and had a lot of knitting needles. These needles hibernated in a long, metal tube through the year, coming out only in October. They would play with bundles of colourful wool and go back in. I got hold of the two heaviest needles. I hit the rim of the bowls and made *Ting Tung* sounds similar to the ones the musician had done. In about fifteen minutes, I had mastered this `anootha' instrument. I cleared the glass bowls, placed them back on the shelf and went to bed. I lay there thinking about how inanely simple it was to be on national television, and drifted off to sleep.

The next morning, I told mom about my plan to carry the bowls and needles to school on Monday. She looked at me strangely and remarked that I had no dearth of ideas to make an idiot of myself. I explained the bigness of my plan. She countered that I couldn't be serious about playing an instrument I had heard of just the previous afternoon. I insisted that I was a natural and that I had already practised. She finally gave in after telling me several times that if I cracked even one of the bowls, she would crack my head. Joyfully, I pulled out my glass notes from the showcase. I didn't want anyone in class to think that this was a random instrument, a stray set that I had picked up and which anyone could do with equal aplomb. I wanted the public to believe that I had been secretly mastering a rare instrument for years. With a sketch pen, I gave them their profound identities – *Sa Re Ga Ma Pa Da Ni.*

On Monday morning, I woke up earlier than usual. With great caution, I wrapped the bowls in Deccan Herald, put them in a bag along with the knitting needles and went to school. I hid it in the Staff Room, behind the cupboard where the tabla set lay. I was twitchy through the day. With great difficulty, I stopped myself from telling anyone about it. My hidden musical talent had to equal or even surpass Saleem's. No one had put Saleem and tabla together but at least we all knew what it looked and sounded like. This inventive combination of `Jaltarangam and Anand' had to create a storm. At 5:30 pm, the school cleared out except for students in various classrooms rehearsing various performances. Even Miss asked us to begin our rehearsals while she cleared up some work. I filled my water bottle, picked up the hidden bag and entered the classroom as our group was assembling. The girls stood in front, the boys behind and Saleem sat down. I smiled at everyone and with great modesty, told them that their heads were about to explode. The group stared as I sat next to Saleem, unwrapped the glass bowls and expertly filled them with water. Every day in school, the teachers would frequently yell, `I want pin drop silence.' Here it was. In all the years of MIHPS, there had never been pin drop silence like this. Being the school leader, I couldn't be questioned easily by the others. Furthermore, the group wasn't sure if this was one more of Even Miss's surprises. I joked that this act looked like kheer being served but in fact, it was a rare instrument called *jaltarangam*. Imagine `pin drop silence' to the power of seven! I broke the silence with the knitting needles on *Sa Re Ga Ma*. I looked up behind and saw confused expressions. The next instant, all of them turned towards the door and I followed their gaze. Even Miss stared at me like a goat, with flared nostrils. Rather, she looked like a ram given her size and overbearing personality. I was unnerved but then I knew that the only way to combat confusion was with conviction.

Me: *Good evening, Miss. I am playing jaltarangam.*

Minutes passed, feeling like months. In her booming voice, she asked me to clear the bowls and join the group at the back. I hadn't been yelled at often in school and this was humiliating. Attempting to sound assured, I told her that with a bit more of group rehearsal, we could create history in school. She thundered that I would become history if I didn't get up that very minute. Feeling disappointed, angry and awkward, I carried the seven musical notes to the window and emptied them.

In the evening, I lied to mom that everyone had loved the idea but as a group, we had concurred that the instrument didn't go well with the song we had chosen that year. She checked the bowls for cracks and arranged them back on the shelf.

Our idiotic rehearsals continued. We practised hard and won the competition. Saleem made a big impression. But we fell well short of blowing the school apart with *Ting Tung*.

. . . .

(25)

RELIGIOUS STAMP(EDE)

I had just crossed the middle school milestone. Class VII was over and the holidays held their open arms out at me. Dad and mom said that we would leave for Bangalore in ten days. A part of every Summer holidays was spent at his elder brother's house in Malleswaram. Dad had 13 siblings and he was the youngest. This uncle, Ranganath Rao, was a highly qualified geologist and had done extremely well. Naturally, the large family pivoted around his house. Close to Cluny Convent in Malleswaram, he owned a big factory called Alminrock Fabrics, meaning all minerals and rocks. Here, he had every conceivable type of stone on earth. Most of them were academic specimens. His core business dealt with cutting and polishing stones into precise laboratory samples that got used as teaching aids in colleges across a few countries. He ran a healthy, reputable business. Given his hard work and good fortune, he had amassed a lot of money. He had a large bungalow on the 16th cross and this was our Family Central. All our relatives who ran into the hundreds, often assembled here.

Uncle Ranganath's wife, my aunt Susheela, was the real force in the family. While he kept himself busy with business, she oversaw the running of the family, hers as well as the extended. She was the matriarch, with strong opinions and decisions made on behalf of hundreds of relatives. She conducted the clan in an extremely sensible and pious way. In other words, she was God's real daughter. She had submitted herself so much to Him that at times, I was sure He craved for some solitude. Her entire life was spent organizing pujas, going to temples and singing devotional songs. She had only stopped short of converting the house into a public place of worship. Round the year, all festivities and sacred functions (thread & death ceremonies, *ekadashi, nagapanchami,* full moon day, no moon day, lunar eclipse, solar eclipse, *upakarma*) and a hundred other rituals got carried out. By a miserly estimate, this house hosted rituals on 200 days of the year. Since early childhood, I had always spent a part of my holidays here. Mom and dad would bring Sriram and me to Bangalore, deposit us, spend a couple of days and go back. After 2-3 weeks, both or one of them would come back for us. I would meet cousins, run errands for aunt and make myself useful for my uncle. I would spend a lot of time in his factory, sit with various workers, constantly pester them to let me grind stones or polish them. Once in a while, they would relent and my unsure hands would butt into their intricate process.

On this particular trip, my stint in Bangalore was in its happy routine. One day, the house slowly started turning upside down. There was frenetic activity that started with shopping. My aunt piled me into the station wagon along with many empty cloth bags. This Willys station wagon bearing the registration number MYS 99 was one of a handful in the whole of Karnataka. It was military green and took up half the road. As the driver manoeuvred it to Malleswaram 8th Cross market, Susheela aunty cross-checked the longest shopping list I'd ever seen. I inferred that a massive family function was around the corner. We bought quintals of vegetables and fruits, sacks of rice, dal and flour, enormous quantities of cashews and raisins etc. We cleared out stocks of our regular supplier, and that a few others fortunate enough to be situated on either side of him. On the way back, I kept looking at her with question marks in my eyes. She told me that one of the most revered and renowned Swamijis was coming home a few days later to perform one of the most sacred and sought-after pujas. Special cooks would arrive and cook food in the backyard for hundreds. After the puja, the drawing room would be cleared out and 50-60 people would feast at a time. To me, every puja meant the same and I never bothered about any of them. At the appropriate time, the elders always instructed me to do certain things and I followed.

On the appointed day, the sun woke up and blinked twice in surprise. Like me, it was also stumped by the bigness of the occasion. My aunt had given so much to our religion that the head priest of one of the big establishments was impressed enough to undertake this journey. As a devotee of martial arts, this was the equivalent of Bruce Lee visiting my house. That morning, nearly a hundred relatives assembled. The great Swamiji landed with his retinue. A fire was manufactured in the drawing room. He sat in front of it and in a loud voice, uttered the most sacred mantras. All the family elders sat or stood around in reverence. Some of them joined the Swamiji in his utterances every now and then. I wanted to be in the factory but mom stared me down and ordered me to be a part of this once-in-a-lifetime event. I stood in one corner, nestled between two uncles. To me, all the Swamiji's chants sounded the same. Everyone else was agog with excitement. I guess the only other thing that found this boring was the fire. It kept dancing vaguely in odd directions looking for respite but the Swamiji would stoke it at regular intervals. After what seemed like ages, lunch was served. I had managed to survive this tedium and looked forward to my trip to the factory. That's when dad told me that the main event would start soon.

The sleepy fire was poked back to life and the mantras resumed. There was a flurry of activity among the massive gathering. Each uncle sought out his respective wife and took some money. This was to hand over to the Swamiji when each one went up for individual blessings. Now every uncle stood with a bared torso. People from the neighbourhood started collecting outside the house. Every brahmin in Malleswaram and the surrounding areas had heard of the Swamiji's presence by now. Hundreds left their offices midway and started queuing up on the street. Though it was a private screening, my aunt's largesse was such that everyone was welcomed. At one point, I stepped out of the house and saw the line. It dwarfed the queue outside Kalpana Talkies for a Dr.Rajkumar release. The Swamiji had surely promised a special act and I had no clue what that was to be.

At half past three, the chanting stopped and people got into their positions. All the men in order of seniority moved closer to the Swamiji. The women flanked to one side and all the cousins were jumbled together. The climax was about to start, and I was dying to witness it. I peered through two sets of thighs for a clear view of the Swamiji and the fire. From inside his bag, he pulled out two silver rods, each one the size of a small carrot. A collective gasp went around the assembly. These were undoubtedly precious in value but priceless in the currency of holy items. He held the broad sides of the rods into the fire and started chanting. Everyone's eyes were transfixed on the Swamiji; mine were on the silver rods. The next instant, one of my oldest uncles stepped forward. Though he was frail and mild mannered, he stood with the poise of a Spartan. The Swamiji stamped my uncle's body with the sizzling silver rods, not once but five times - once on each upper arm and thrice on his chest. My uncle didn't wince, not even once.

Me: *Ammmmmmmmaaaaaaaaaaaaaaaaaaaa!*

I went hysterical. I didn't understand what was wrong with either the Swamiji or my uncle. Mom was somewhere among the women. A few of my older cousins asked me to shut up. One of the uncles held me gently and said in a mellifluous voice,

Uncle: *One rod has the impression of a shankha (conch shell) and the other, a chakra (wheel).*

He said it like a bakery guy describing some exotic sweets on his shelf. I wanted to say various unmentionables but was so shocked by this heinous act that no words came out. As I watched in pure horror, a second uncle got scarred and two more stepped forward for their turn. And then an older cousin who was still not a full adult was asked to step ahead. He got two stampings, one on each upper arm. He contorted his body in pain and staggered back. The Swamiji shoved the silver rods back into the fire. The uncle next to me explained the pattern in a voice as comforting as that of Yesudas.

Uncle: *The silver rods go back into the fire after every fifth stamping. When the Swamiji pulls it out, the first three are reserved for us, grown-ups.*

I heard this and didn't want to grow up ever.

Uncle: *We take five stampings, but this isn't mandatory. It's just our devotion. Once the rods cool a bit, either the women or the younger ones get just two on their upper arms. And the cycle repeats. We are lucky and blessed. Stay here. Your turn will come.*

My brain had shrunk so badly that I took time to process this. And then I thought of the hundreds outside the house. They had to wait for hours, pay *dakshina*, get scarred and go home. What possessed them to do this was simply beyond me.

I ran, squeezing through the cluster of my crazed family. Some of the uncles noticed and pointed in my direction. Mom, dad and a few cousins charged after me. I ran like a greyhound and reached the crossing to MES College, which seemed like a safe distance. Panting hard, I wept in fright. By now, dad and the others closed in on me. I could have run farther but that felt a little scary. Not the fear of getting lost but of rebelling totally against the family. So, I just stood with my legs apart, trying hard not to pee. Twenty minutes of firm talk alternated with soothing words. They promised me that I would be the very last one before the Swamiji packed up. They said that by then, there would be no fire and only ash. Howling like a puppy about to be butchered, I walked back with them. Most of the family had got their shots and now strangers were barging in. Dad and an uncle held me firmly, lifted and placed me in front of the Swamiji. We had cut the queue.

Uncle: *Family avnu. Miss aag hoythu.*

(He's from the family. He got missed.)

The Swamiji smiled and lifted the rods. I went into a living version of rigor mortis. Twenty minutes later, I was in one of the bedrooms with some of my cousins and uncles. I had no recollection of the time in between. I looked at my two shots. Honestly, they didn't hurt as much as I had imagined probably because I had been so stressed that various organs in my body had blown their fuses, including parts of the brain that registered pain. The Swamiji packed up at 6:30 in the evening. Hundreds of people in the queue were turned back; they went home feeling accursed and disappointed. All my relatives thanked Susheela aunty for this most blessed experience.

A year later, when Summer holidays came calling, I told dad and mom that I wasn't going to Malleswaram.

. . . .

(PART 2)

FULL PANT TALES FROM SHIMOGA

(26)

SNAKE GOURD

Growing up in Shimoga had its jollies but was also a handicap. It was the proverbial well and all of us were toads. During holidays, most of us visited relatives in the big cities and got our taste of the cultures we wanted to be in. To us, Bangalore seemed like New York and Mysore carried the vibe of California. Our reality was 'mofussil to metropolitan and back.' I was clear that moving ahead in life, it would be the reverse. And so, I constantly looked for influences that would take us from bronze to gold.

In the Summer holidays of 1985, I went to Bangalore for a couple of weeks to stay with an aunt in Jayanagar. Rani, my cousin from Mysore, two years younger, also decided to come down. I couldn't have asked for more. We were extremely close and had endless things to talk about. Rani was quite a looker and for her age, she was considered fast. Any girl who interacted with a stranger of the opposite sex received this label. Even at her age, she had quite a few boyfriends. Having a boyfriend meant walking down two streets, looking around furtively for any known faces and then sneaking in a 5-minute conversation with the boy. And doing this every single day around an appointed time. Even when Rani would visit Bangalore for a few days, she managed to find these 5-minute conversationalists within a day or two of being in a new neighbourhood. This time around, it was a two-week trip, and I had no doubt that she would have a veritable hoard of five-minute talkers at her disposal. A day or two later, Rani and I had walked to the end of the street to have *pani-puri* when we saw a group of four guys. They looked the same age as me but were infinitely cooler. One of them took a fancy to Rani and vice versa. So while I played guardian, Rani and the boy chatted. His name was Joy. As Rani was getting to know him better, I had already fallen head over heels in love with Joy. Not the boy but the name. Over the next two weeks, we met this gang everyday but never for more than five minutes each day. The fabulous foursome consisted of Joy, Ashley, Rohan and Bruce. At the end of our trip, Rani went back to Mysore and I headed back to my well.

Every Summer break, I carried back some influence of the big city. A few years earlier, it had been Commando comics. Another year, it was a new song, Funky Town. Yet another time, it was the name of a shoe brand that was the most happening, RoadStar. On the first day of school, I usually spoke to my gang about the life and times of our counterparts in the big cities and urged all of us to be like them. This year was a bonanza of a deeper kind. I had never met a gang that had such arresting names. Agreed, Rohan wasn't so hot but Joy? Ashley? Bruce? I reflected upon the names in our gang: Vishak Acharya, Deepak Shetty, Narasimha Murthy, Amoghavarsha, Sumanth, Nijaguna, Anand...BAH! As if growing up in Shimoga wasn't uncool enough!

The next morning, we assembled at Vishak's house. It was the first day of our new term and all of us were back from our holidays. This week would go in exchanging vacation stories but first, there was something crucial that I had to lay down.

Me: Vishak, ivathinda neenu Joy, Narsimha Bruce, Shetty Clive and naanu Ashley!

(Vishak, from today you are Joy, Narasimha is Bruce, Shetty is Clive and I am Ashley!)

I admit that Joy was my first love but over two weeks, Ashley had grown on me like a tumour. I had reserved this name for myself back in Bangalore itself. Rohan wasn't happening and so I had thought of Clive. Vishak Acharya, Narasimha Murthy and Deepak Shetty just didn't get it. They looked at me like the toads they were. I explained that we needed to have cool names and how plebian ours sounded. I asked them to visualize how sexy we would appear yelling these names in the course of a cricket match.

Me: *Bruce, swalpa pace haaku!*

(Bruce, pace it up!)

In my head, just this comment added confidence to the proceedings rather than,

Me: *Narasimha, pace haaku!*

(Narasimha, pace it up!)

This sounded like asking Gundappa Vishwanath to design sexy clothes. There was confused silence. I laboured the point that no hairstyle, RoadStars or jeans of any kind could do much, if our core uncoolness didn't change. I even spoke economics arguing that to make Narasimha Murthy hip would cost a lot of money whereas a Bruce or Ashley in torn clothes would still appear groovy. They kept staring at me. Finally,

Narasimha: *Ninige yaavdho kanthri nayi kachchir beku!*

(You must've been bitten by a stray dog!)

Deepak Shetty: *Ee naak hesru thogondu underwear alli itko!*

(Take these four names and shove it inside your underwear!)

Vishak: *Anna, nam gang hinge irli. Neenu avara gang serko. Hogolo!*

(Brother, let our gang stay the way it is. You go and join their gang. Get lost!)

I was stunned. I had been the social and cultural gang leader for years and had never been questioned, let alone a mutiny. We were thick friends and I really cared for them. I didn't want to let their stupidity affect their future. So I proposed a bargain.

Me: *Tension beda. It's ok. Nim hesru hunge irli. Nanna maathra Ashley antha kareeri.*

(It's ok. No need to stress. You stick to your names. But call me

Ashley.)
I was sure that after a few days, they would discover the zing of a name and then plead for their liberation as well.
Deepak: *Ninna tondekaayi antha karitheevi. Seri na?*
(We'll call you a gherkin. Is that fine?)
Narasimha: *Illa, padwalkaayi!*
(No, snake gourd is better.)
This was as random as it was instinctive. They merely reeled off names of a couple of vegetables, both of which tasted awful but more importantly, sounded foul and uncool. As we cycled to school, the three toads guffawed all the way.

· · · · · · · **●** ● **●** ● ● ● · · · ·

(27)

BANANA TO BABYLON

By the time we were in the 8th standard, we had read every Secret Seven, Famous Five, Malory Towers, Hardy Boys and Nancy Drew, including one disappointing combination of the last two. Each series opened up different possibilities in our heads. After our Secret Four days in the fourth standard, our adventures had cooled off a bit. The spark re-kindled when we met Vivek who was a year senior to us in school. His parents were doctors, and he came into our gang through Narasimha, whose dad was also a reputed doctor in Shimoga. Vivek's nickname was Banana as he was very fond of them. He was quite an oddball and did some strange things. Yet, he was well read and bright though somewhat nerdy and terrible at cricket. Being a year older, he had also read all the books that we had. One word that fascinated him was `camouflage' and he managed to infect us.

Three months into our friendship, on a Saturday afternoon, six of us cycled a few kilometres to the outskirts of Shimoga. We stopped on a small road flanked by bushes and paddy fields. There was a sprinkling of tiny villages around. Oxen and bullock carts were common traffic. Infrequently, a well-to-do villager passed by on a TVS 50 or a Suvega. Banana led us to a small channel of water. It flowed lazily ten feet below us, passing under the road through a large pipe. Bushes, creepers and sporadic dense foliage lined its banks. We slithered down the slope with Banana's Raleigh cycle, put it down on its side, covered it with leafy vines and filled the gaps with dried leaves. Back on the road, we looked at it from various angles. Not a sliver was visible. It looked as if professionals had camouflaged it. Satisfied with our efforts and skill, we felled some tamarind with stones, sat by the side of the road and savoured the sourness. We didn't have to wait long. Soon enough, a villager was walking in our direction. We hailed him and pointing in the direction of the cycle, said that we had just spotted a humongous snake below. The villager stared closely at the spot. We kept pointing at the cycle, exclaiming that we could still see parts of the snake. He stared with intensity and then muttered that big snakes were a common occurrence here but they bore no harm. Lighting up a bidi, he carried on. We exchanged high-fives with much gusto. Passing the Villager Test was a huge kick.

A few weekends later, we cycled out of Shimoga on a similar trip. After another resounding victory, we decided to cycle through the nearest village before heading home. This held no more than 30-odd huts and a couple of petty shops. Most villagers were in the fields. Some old men sat around smoking bidis, a few kids played while some people were busy collecting water at a hand pump. This five-minute cycle ride through the village stirred something deep inside me. A couple of days later, I told Vishak that I desired to do something and would need his help. For the first time in all our years, I had used the word `desire' and not `scheme'. It was unusual and Vishak didn't know what to make of it. I told him that we were now grown up, well-to-do and it was time we did our bit for humanity. I reminded him of the village we had cycled through and said that we ought to do something for the villagers. Half an hour later, Vishak and I were in the middle of the village. We stopped at a few places and observed. The kids were dirty and playing silly games in the mud. I asked Vishak about his bags of childhood toys. He replied that they were all in his attic. They were of no use to him or us. In an instant, we agreed to distribute the toys among these kids and spread joy. We pedalled back and filled our bags with an assortment of toys: plastic balls, tops, cars, a London double-decker bus, animal figurines, toy guns etc. Talking about more grandiose plans of social welfare, we cycled back to the village and stopped a few feet from a bunch of kids. The oldest must have been eight and the youngest, two. We could see the villagers working in the fields, not more than fifty feet away. Pulling out a few toys, we cheerfully called out to the kids. They kept staring at us. No one moved. I had imagined that the first sight of a spinning top or a gun would cause a scramble. I kept insisting that these toys were for them, and for free. I then gently tossed a plastic gun towards them. It fell between the kids and us. I urged them to pick it up. All of a sudden, the oldest girl yelled. We were taken aback. The next instant, a few villagers screamed from the fields and started running towards us. It suddenly dawned on us that the girl's shout was a cry for rescue. There had been reports of village kids being lured with chocolates and kidnapped. We had been mistaken for child-lifters. We jumped on our cycles and fled, easing up only after entering the safety of Shimoga. Panting and laughing at this cruel twist of fate, we parted.

The next day, I told Vishak that I had noticed the absence of something else in the village. It lacked easy and clean drinking water. After discussing a bit, we decided that the village needed a borewell.

Both of us knew nothing about it and so we landed up at Shimoga Central Library. It was a huge place with a collection of tens of thousands of books. Anybody could go in and browse but one had to be a member to borrow the books. It was usually filled with several college students referencing myriad topics, and some retired people reading the day's papers. The librarian sat at the entrance, which was also the exit. Vishak and I walked in, browsed for a bit, and found a stack of books on borewells. Picking the one that looked promising, we made our way to a table. It had lots of information but wasn't easy to understand. We didn't have ample time to write down all the useful chapters and so decided to come back another day. As Vishak was placing the book back on the rack, I suddenly felt that the library could and should sacrifice one book towards our noble cause. I looked around and spotted no one. More importantly, no one could spot us. I quickly pulled out a thinner book on borewells and shoved it under my pant waistline. With my shirt on the outside, I checked for any visible signs of a bulge. It looked well camouflaged. We walked out and the librarian didn't spare us a look. Later, we spoke about what could have happened if I had been caught. The consequences would have been dire. Vishak said that the theft was a stupid gamble because we didn't need the book. Our idea was not to build the borewell ourselves, anyway. We just needed a rough understanding of the technology and the cost so that we could plan the project and the finances. We made discreet enquiries with our dads telling them that one of the teachers had posed this in class. His doctor and my railway guard scratched their heads and gave us vague replies. After a few more days of checking with sundry people, we arrived at a ballpark cost of thirty thousand rupees. That was a huge sum but not totally out of bounds. Vishak and I discussed various options to raise this kind of money.

After some thinking, I arrived at what seemed like a good idea. I decided to write a novel about us. In my head, it would take a week to put down our stories. Within 2-3 weeks, the book would be out and we could definitely raise enough money to get the borewell done, and also have some left over for other causes. Vishak agreed wholeheartedly. We spent the next two hours discussing all the incidents that qualified to go into the book. We reminisced about our childhood and rolled with laughter over various episodes. The more we chatted, the more we realized that the book would do extremely well. Vishak and I had started writing poetry by then. Our ability to convey complex thoughts and also consistently find words that rhymed, surprised us. Since I had a keener memory, I was to be the lead writer. I would parcel out little incidents to Vishak and he would fill those out. Within five days, we would be done with the book and spend a day matching our writing styles. A week later, it would go in for printing.

Our larger purpose and the imminent task were both divine and charged us up. I had memories behind and a purpose ahead. I went berserk and finished 56 notebook pages in three days. I showed them to Vishak and we picked out portions that could be elaborated on. He started work on these sections. We used to sit in one of the last benches in class and easily did the work while class was in progress. As we neared the completion of our book, we decided to tell Banana Vivek about it. He was the most qualified to guide us through the next steps. We hid the borewell angle from him because he sometimes reacted strangely to perfectly normal things. We pitched it as a mere literary pursuit and stated that we would be getting into printing soon. Banana went bananas. It seemed that this was something he was also keen upon. He asked us many questions, held his head, thought hard, took in every detail of our endeavour and then started blowing it apart. He rambled about Shakespeare, Eliot, Mark Twain, Enid Blyton, Wodehouse as well as a few others we were clueless about. He called us fools for thinking that this was child's play. He hypnotised us into believing that publishing a book took anywhere between 3-9 years. At the end of his rant, he asserted that our route to money or fame was as fickle as fireflies. Vishak and I thought about this profound line for sometime. We had come to him with hopes of encouragement and expertise, not unfathomable vehemence and exposition. After some hesitation, I told Banana that fireflies were actually steadfast. He laughed scornfully and seeded more doubts in my mind. There was no doubt that he knew better. We bought into him with the naivete of babies. His conviction and body language crushed our spirit. Vishak and I decided to pursue writing at a later stage when we would have more time on our hands.

For now, we had to quickly figure out an alternative to raise money for the borewell. I thought hard and came up trumps. The plan was a group effort, one that looked easy and promising. We were all natural, avid cyclists. I decided that we would cycle across Karnataka and raise funds. It would take us a couple of weeks but would also be great fun. But unlike writing a book, this came with costs. We had to halt every evening and needed food and accommodation. Banana's parents were active members of the Lions Club. We felt that the Club would be delighted to support our cause and take up the necessary arrangements. Vishak and I discussed the plan in detail and concluded that this was a fail-safe idea. We decided to approach Banana so that he could move it up to his parents, who would in turn move it up to the committee. Banana's parents had a large clinic on the ground floor and lived above. Vishak and I went up the stairs, crossed the large terrace and knocked on his door. He was in one of his weird moods and didn't even invite us in. Standing at the door, we told him about our scheme. He said `*Thoo!*' and shut the door on us. We were mighty hurt and angry. This was no way to treat social workers. But the vehemence with which he had reacted to our scheme made us feel that maybe, we had been naïve again. Having our backs broken twice within ten days crippled our heads and hearts, and we went back to playing cricket. The village, the borewell, the novel and the cycling expedition lay behind in ruins.

About a month later, Vishak and I were rummaging for something in his house when we came across the borewell book. We flipped through it and started reminiscing when a fertile idea wafted into our heads. We had become literary in the past few years and had at one point, spoken seriously about starting our own circulating library. A few others in the gang had also been quite keen, most notably Amogha. And going by the borewell book escapade, starting a library wasn't so difficult. The next day, we shared the plan with the rest of the gang and ended up with an enthusiastic ensemble. We needed about 250 books to announce our library. Our own collection stood at 156. We had work to do.

Vishak's terrace was chosen to be the library. Over a weekend, we cut up coloured chart papers and made our library cards. We worked out a tier-system depending on the profitability of the customer and hence made cards in various colours. We first indexed Vishak's set of books. Amogha had a healthy collection of comics and Deepak Shetty was an avid collector of sports magazines. We just needed a lot more novels to start. I shared with Amogha how easily I had walked out with a book from the Shimoga Central Library. He laughed like a compulsive thief. This library had its share of novels, on two large racks in one corner. That Saturday, four of us landed there. While the other two kept watch, Amogha and I managed to grab a book each. Ten minutes later, we strode out like a commando force. It had turned out to be a piece of cake. Over the next three months, we pillaged the library. With each successful run, our confidence soared. From one book each, we started walking out with two apiece. We ran this routine a few times without being spotted or stopped. After the third run, even Vishak managed to whisk one out. We were getting closer to our target count but also felt a growing sense of urgency. After all, patience was the biggest adversary of enthusiasm. We decided on one final, daring run.

Amogha's dad was a lecturer in Sahyadri College and naturally owned a couple of black coats. Amogha sneaked a coat out of his house and wore it on Vishak's terrace. It stopped a few centimetres above his ankle. He looked like a bear and a satellite could have picked him up in an instant. We laughed and decided against it. All of a sudden, he turned hostile. He insisted that it fit him perfectly and didn't look odd at all. He mother-promised us that in case he got caught, he would not give us away. With this absurd bear in tow, we walked into the library looking nerve-wracked. An 8th standard boy wearing a black coat that reached his ankles was a dead give-away. But neither the librarian nor any of the others even raised their heads and looked in our direction. They were all living-dead, possibly because *Ugadi* had just got over and all of them must have had litres of *gasgase payasa*. There could be no other explanation. Amogha stuffed in 8 novels while I picked up 3 with just my shirt to cover them. Vishak chipped in with 1, Deepak packed 1 and within ten minutes, we walked out with 13 books. Our collection had swelled close to 250 novels by now. Commando comics were a rage and we needed to have a collection of those as well. They were available in plenty at a private circulating library. Three of us were members and went there almost every day. This was so small that the owner sitting at the entrance could touch everyone inside the library. Our kleptomania skills had been honed to perfection. From here, we managed to lift over 35 Commando comics. We were set and only needed an appropriate name. Each of us had ideas and a collective choice became a tough task. After much discussion, we wrote down the shortlisted names:

1. BOOKWORMS BOOK HOUSE

2. STORYTELLERS CLUB

3. TAAT - Two At A Time

(Some libraries allowed members to borrow only one book at a time. We thought that increasing this number was a good incentive.)

4. SBLS - Shimoga Book Lovers Society

(There was something so worldly about calling it a society instead of a library.)

5. LATEST LIBRARY

(This could potentially draw lots of customers. In case someone asked for the latest novel and we didn't have it, we could always say that we were so named because we were the most recent one in Shimoga.)

6. BABYLON

(This had no relevance but sounded so grandiose that we just couldn't get it out of contention. Vishak and I were particularly taken up by this. In fact, Vishak made the library card and the two of us discussed with much enthusiasm that once we finalised on this name, we would re-write the card on the lines of Hammurabi's Code.)

We could not arrive at a consensus, so we decided to start the library and agree on a name soon. The most obvious thing was to spread the news in school. But only those who lived close to Vishak's house would land up. The others had libraries in their own localities. All of us who lived close to Vishak's house were co-owners. We had to have other people in our neighbourhood as members. On either side of Vishak's house was large empty spaces. A main road ran in front of it. Beyond that lay PWD Quarters, which didn't have many readers. Stretching behind his

Rules

1) members have to show this identification card which is provided to them while getting or returning book.

2) members can exchang the books only once in a day

3) if the book is not returned by next day double charge is taken

4) if the book is not returned entire charge of the book is taken

5) no opinions should be written in books

Date ——————— Signature :
V _ k A h a

Timings :—
      evening 5.30 to 7.00
                              P.T.O

house was Tank Mohalla that had people more likely to be booked for petty crimes. We had a severe location disadvantage. After much promotion, we managed 5 members who asked for inaugural discounts. Every evening after school, we had to cart 300-odd books to the terrace and arrange them. Around 6:40 pm, we had to lug them back to Vishak's room. With each passing day, the venture made less sense and after a fortnight, we called for a committee meeting and voted to close it down.

· · · · · · · · · · · · · · · · · · ·

(28)

OH GOD!

I will start with a bold and reckless statement: I had come close to hating God! We didn't have any personal enmity and led our own lives doing our own things. But since I belonged to a god-fearing, pious Kannadiga family, I was told to submit myself to Him every day. To be fair to my parents, they didn't make me do anything extraordinary. I knew families who were so fervently religious that I would have discarded them if God had put me in their midst. At home, I was asked to do nothing more than a one-minute supplication before the deity every morning. This was the least that was asked of anyone but to me, it felt like a big encumbrance. For dad, this was the most significant thing each morning.

Dad: *Ananda, vidya kelu, buddhi kelu, aamele thanks hel bidu. Ashte!* (Ask for knowledge, intelligence, and thank Him. That's all!)

I got this perfectly. I had the wisdom to realize that asking for knowledge and intelligence was better than asking for marks or money. If one got marks, one would make money. If one had money, one didn't need marks. I advised those who had neither to ask specifically for one or both. I always scored well and so this wasn't relevant to me. What I didn't get was the pointless bit about asking Him every day. After all, He was right up there. You said something to Him once and He would remember it for life.

152

The world walked around saying that someone had been dealt a wretched life because God hadn't forgotten his crimes and follies from his previous birth. If that was indeed the case, what was the point about these daily reminders? And so, this one-minute ritual threw up far too many questions with no real answers.

When I graduated from shorts to pants, I stopped this ritual altogether. By now, I had the gumption to question dad. One day, he remarked that I had become too big for my shorts, but I dare never think that I am bigger than Him. This was below the waistline and couldn't go unchallenged.

Me: *Appa, devru ell idhaare?*

(Dad, where's God?)

Dad looked at me queerly. In these matters, he couldn't be smart.

Dad: *Devru ella kade idhaare.*

(God is everywhere.)

I had tricked him into making a wrong chess move.

Me: *Andhre, toilet allu idhare. Naanu toilet alli puje maad theeni.*

(Which means, in the toilet too. So, I'll pray in the toilet.)

Dad twitched involuntarily. On this topic, logic was blasphemy.

Dad: *Maad beda! But dayavittu huchhuch aage maathaad beda.*

(Don't pray! But please don't talk such rot.)

I pushed him further saying that I had no issues praying if he could give me a logical answer. He walked off in utter pain. That day, he spent an extra minute beseeching Him to offer knowledge and intelligence to his offspring. With age, I was turning from a good brahmin boy to an agnostic to an atheist. I was now in Class IX and rapidly moving up the scale. One day, I was reflecting upon these metaphysical issues when I recalled a past incident. It made me guffaw at the sheer idiocy of the act.

I had finished my sixth standard and Sriram was done with his ninth. Summer holidays had begun. Days were spent playing marbles; the game of the season that year. One day, while having lunch,

Mom: *If you write `Sriram Jairam Jai Jai Ram' one-crore-and-one-times and put it in the hundi of the Raghavendra Swami Mutt, you will be rid* *of every sin.*

I stared at mom wordlessly for the next three minutes. This was a stunning piece of news! Where and why had she hidden this magic potion all these years? There was something so conclusive yet surreal about this proposal. Both Sriram and I felt the same pull towards something for the first time in our lives. We raced through our lunch and pulled out fresh notebooks. With the now attainable *mukti* in our sights, we put pen to paper. We spent hours doing this every day. We continued to play marbles but for lesser time. We even started losing badly. Our minds were constantly on this long journey towards *moksha*. Naturally, it became very competitive. We started waking up fifteen minutes earlier and sleeping twenty minutes later. Some days, I would get up and see Sriram already rushing ahead with his lines. Our bath times got shortened. Wherever we could gain a few minutes over the other, we scribbled a few more lines. Sriram was a slow eater but now he finished at the same time I did. When he went to the toilet or for his bath, I would flip open his book to compare our progress. Each page held 32 lines and he was ahead by 7 pages. Of course, my handwriting was much neater but he was faster. Also, he had an advantage. The first word of the line was his name and obviously he had practised it far more than me. I resolved to put in extra hours. There was no way his book could go into the *hundi* first.

As the days passed, the path to salvation grew tiresome. So, we started doing what anyone would do in this situation. We broke the task up into more manageable pieces. In the mornings, we would fill several pages with only `Sriram'. The afternoons were reserved for `Jairam'. In the nights, we would sleepily fill in `Jai Jai Ram'. Then, we broke this up day-of-the-week wise: Monday for *Sriram,* Tuesday for *Jairam* and so on. Another trick we employed was to jump a few pages ahead and write down the full sentence. This acted as a milestone and then we sped towards it. After several days and nights, this project became mind numbing. One can't keep writing the same thing over and over again. Repetition works in some places but falls apart elsewhere. For instance, I could eat papads every day and find the same joy each time. But this pursuit was – *Aiyo! God Save Me!* Honestly, I had no idea what a crore meant and how long this would take. It had been a week and a half, and I had crossed 18,000 lines, an insane 562 pages. Sriram's count stood at 21,000. I was sick of it by now. I sat down and did a bit of math. Using simple ratio and proportion, I realized that at this rate, it would take me 15 years more. Once school resumed, this rate would come down miserably. In all practicality, it seemed that I would have to devote nearly 34 years of my life to writing the line over and over again. I would start working someday, get married, have kids and this monkey would still be on my back. That was a serious waste of a life. God would never forgive me for squandering one *avatar* of his, over this. I know people said that attaining moksha wasn't easy but when I had embarked on this, it had seemed like a short cut. A sense of futility rose, my interest waned and the pace slackened. On the 15th day, the auspicious day of *purnima*, I put down my pen. By now, I had realized the plot: if one kept at this, he would have no time to sin whatsoever and thereby attain *moksha*. I decided to cut down on sinning but not on ruining my life. With no one chasing him, Sriram also started tottering and came to a halt a few days later.

Then there was this other ritual that used to make me throw up, literally. Every year, a brahmin is supposed to discard his old *janivaara* (sacred thread) and don a new one. This eventful day is called *upakarma*. Dad had been doing this for years, and years later, Sriram joined the ranks after his *upanayana* (thread ceremony). This ceremony was usually carried out in early childhood but Sriram underwent his when he was about fifteen. He had now entered the *brahmacharya* phase, as per the Hindu way of life. Dad was a *grihasta*. I had precociously jumped to the third stage, *vanaprasta* (forest dweller or hermit in semi-retirement). I was regularly climbing trees and spending time in the pumpset. On this auspicious day of *upakarma*, hordes of brahmins made their way to the Raghavendra Swami Mutt. After the thread replacement, dad would get back by noon, but never alone. He always came back with three small balls of rice, one for each of us at home. These balls of rice were modest in size, roughly equivalent to that of a small marble. Truth be told, I would have swallowed a marble dipped in cyanide, with glee. These rice balls used to be dipped in cow's urine. This is a redundancy, but they stank. The religious side of this ritual escapes me but each year, I would be given the healthful argument: cow's urine was not just 'very' but 'extremely' good for health. Mom and dad were not exaggerative people but, on this day, they always spoke in superlatives. I always told them that swallowing a small rice ball laced with cow's urine once a year was equivalent to doing pranayam for one day in one's lifetime. I would cry and rant and tell them that I didn't want to swallow urine. Mom would chide me for saying dirty things about God's *prasad*. I would wonder what His punishment tasted like. Every year, I would create a stink but they wouldn't relent. Mom always comforted me saying that I wouldn't even feel it. Without a flinch, she would swallow her portion.

Mom: *Nodu! Gulum antha nungbidu. Ashte!*

(See! Swallow it…gulum. That's all!)

Before you start thinking that Kannada is a silly language, let me clarify that *gulum* and *gutuk* are not our words. Mothers used these sounds to deceive kids that swallowing something, especially a pill or anything rancid, was not a big deal. With no escape routes available, I would *gulum* it, run to the bathroom and rinse my mouth a few hundred times. I did this for the first thirteen years, after which I grew big enough and so did my tantrums.

Temples and pujas drove me mad. Once a year, dad and mom held a *Satyanarayana puja* in the Raghavendra Swami Mutt. This took close to three hours followed by lunch. I always found the lunch delicious, and the puja disgusting. So, I tried a different tact each time to wriggle out of it. One particular year, God gave me a terrific idea but not enough wisdom, as is His norm. He never gives it all.

I was in Class VIII. Dad and mom decided to conduct a *Satyanarayana puja*. Religion and reality mattered equally to them, and so it was booked for a Sunday so that I could attend it without missing school. The puja was scheduled to groan to life at ten in the morning. Dad, mom and Sriram would reach dutifully before time. I was given a little reprieve but strictly instructed to get there by 11:30 am. This leg of the puja required all of us. Not that I had to do anything other than be present to receive multiple blessings as the puja wore on. Sitting cross-legged on the floor for a few hours had never been my sore point. It was the pujari. As far as I was concerned, I couldn't get a word of anything he said, whether he muttered calculus or verses. Every now and then, he would also scratch his buttocks, clad in a dirty loincloth. Then with the same hand, he would give us flower petals and tulsi leaves to bestow on the deity. Funnily, dad was okay with this physical defilement but not with my reasonable questioning. Since I was older now, I could have told them that I didn't feel like attending the puja but realized that this would upset dad. In fact, all my life, I never did anything deliberate to hurt him. At the same time, I had decided that I would skip it somehow. I just had to have a reason much bigger than the puja.

I told them that I was meeting my friends and would land up at the Mutt at the appointed hour. Deepak Shetty, Vishak and I cycled to Narasimha's house. He lived in a big house five minutes from the Mutt. We started playing short cricket in his compound. I kept cribbing throughout about having to leave at some point. Simultaneously, I was thinking of a scheme for a getaway. As Narasimha was playing with my mind with his leg spin, I suddenly stopped batting and jumped. The perfect excuse stared me in the face. At first glance, it seemed foolish but I convinced myself that it would work. Maybe my desperation led me to believe in this dubious plan. I shared my scheme with the three and they no-balled it, saying it was ridiculous and would never work. I was wearing a white t-shirt and Narasimha's compound was lined with bougainvillea plants.

The pinkish-red flowers were in full bloom. I crushed a handful of flowers, added two drops of water and scrubbed them on my t-shirt. They were supposed to leave red stains and look like dried blood. The rest of the scheme was to work out as follows: my parents would start getting fidgety around 11:40 am. They would start cursing me in their heads for not landing up on time. The clock would strike 12 and I would still not arrive. In fact, I wouldn't turn up for the puja at all. They would get angry and then tense. After lunch, they would head home, not knowing what else to do. I would land up at home at three, looking slightly woozy. But before they yelled at me, I would tell them a distressing story:

"Amma, we were playing cricket in Narasimha's house. I was ready to leave for the Mutt and suddenly Narasimha and I collided badly. His head, and you've seen how big it is, banged into my nose and I passed out. My nose wouldn't stop bleeding. Narasimha's dad had to come back from the hospital to tend to me. He specifically told me not to move or raise my head for two hours. I am terribly sorry about the puja, but I had no choice. My t-shirt is also ruined but thank God, at least I am looking better now."

If you are wondering about my daftness, I did think of using red ink and discarded the plan. Any parent of a school-going child will instantly recognize an ink stain. Bougainvillea flowers were a much better punt. But I don't think Narasimha had purebred bougainvillea. After smearing the flowers, my t-shirt definitely looked stained but nothing remotely like dried blood. It just looked dirty in a strange way. The three of them couldn't stop laughing at the improbability of the scheme and now the outcome. It was time to leave and my mind was whirring. The plan had failed miserably, and I couldn't think of anything else. So, I left for the Mutt.

When I entered, the puja was in progress and dad couldn't speak. But he gave me a look that was many times dirtier than my t-shirt. I had walked in looking defiled. Thankfully, I had to take it off. I settled down with a bared torso and a bored look.

· · · · · · · • • • • · • · · · · ·

(29)

VULGAR

After a long night of duty, dad was wearily stepping into the house when he froze at the door. He looked tired and sleepy but more than anything, he looked utterly pained. He just stood there sighing and 'Why?'ing.

It was only 6:45 am but I had been up and active for a while. I was now in the eighth standard and had started keeping odd hours and doing things my way. Disagreements between dad and me had gone up. Perhaps, they had existed all along but hadn't been vocal, as they now were. I was busy at work in the narrow compound of ours, all of three feet wide and ten feet long. He gave a second long look at my handiwork and sighed wearily.
Dad: *Yaako? vulgar aag idhiyappa!*
(Why? It's looking vulgar!)
I put the spanner down and looked at him with wonderment. Of all the words in the English language, he had chosen a pretty strong and surprising word. Given what he was referring to and the time of day, it sounded totally misplaced. I told him to freshen up first and we could then deal with this. Shaking his head as if having lost the fight even before it had begun, he went inside. I looked at the cycle and it looked sexy to me. In this little compound of ours, we used to park our cycles. One was dad's that had been around for nearly as long as Sriram had been.

It was a big, classic Raleigh and had all the things that a good Kannadiga cycle was supposed to: mud guards with flaps, bell, mirror, dark green seat cover, lock, centre stand, carrier. I had learnt cycling on this when I was in the second standard. By the fourth, I had started using it frequently, knowing that in a few years' time, dad would buy me my own. The other cycle in the compound now, also a Raleigh, was mine obviously. To understand its `vulgar' present, a dip into its pristine past is required.

When I was in the fifth standard, my aunt and uncle had come down from Delhi. One evening, my uncle asked me to get dressed and took me to Nehru Road. I thought he would buy me sweets like he usually did. Instead, he took me to the Popular Cycle Mart and asked me to choose a cycle. I reeled with excitement. Sweets to cycle was a crazy leap. He smiled and said that he had decided on this before arriving in Shimoga. That's when the two parts of my brain started their argument. One was the well-grounded, substance-over-style Kannadiga brain. This preferred a big, classic Raleigh just like the one dad had. For decades, the Raleigh had been the embodiment of the perfect Kannada male: strong and silent, responsible, hardworking and long-lasting. It was generally believed that like everyone around, even the Raleigh had a retirement age set at 58 years. Also, it could carry three adults at a time. If you knocked off two people, it could hold ten kilos of rice, three kilos of dal, fruits and vegetables, including a watermelon or a jackfruit, along with a 5-6 year-old kid. In extreme cases, it would carry two big bundles of firewood or even a few gas cylinders. On the other hand, the other part of my brain didn't want anything to do with, anything Kannadiga. This one craved for either a Hero or a BSA sports cycle, preferably in red. The sports cycle didn't have any of the warrior-like qualities of the Raleigh. It looked like it would last for five years, at the most. Only in extreme cases, it would agree to carry two people. But, the BSA had more *shoki* (style). The ends of the handlebars in the Raleigh curved towards the rider and looked old-fashioned. The designers of the BSA had given it handlebars that angled fashionably. It had a much smaller seat for new age, younger people. The older Kannadigas had big buttocks and the Raleigh seat suited them better. I was caught between the two parts of my brain and couldn't decide. I knew dad would be utterly disappointed with me if I picked the BSA. I imagined what he would say.

Dad: *Life threw a great uncle and a great opportunity your way, but you squandered it.*

I think, uncle read my mind.

Uncle: *Appan tarah yochne maadbeda. Ninage yaavdhu beko, thogo.*

(Don't think like your dad. Buy whichever you like.)

After forty minutes of staring at both, I decided on a Raleigh. Uncle looked at me for a good two minutes, an unasked question. I nodded my head vigorously to tell him that it was my decision, and I was sure. On the way home, I felt happy but not joyous. When we reached home, dad was joyous.

Dad: *Volledu, sensible kelsa maad dya.*

(Good. You did a sensible thing.)

With this comment, he hit the nail on the head. I wasn't feeling ecstatic because I had done a sensible thing; nothing beyond that.

The Raleigh and I got through my middle school fairly well. But now, I was in high school. I had become more fashionable, and the Raleigh stuck out like a Kannada medium student. Most of my classmates had sports cycles and some had gone ahead and altered even those. So, the previous day, I had started my alterations and dad was now staring at my handiwork, after freshening up. I had completely undressed the cycle. The mudguards, mirror, chain guard, centre stand, bell, carrier and the lock had been removed. The cycle had lost half its original weight and could race faster. Now, the handlebar pointed towards the sky and made me look taller in this posture. One of the shops sold a black plastic tape which had become a rage among cyclists. I had wound it tightly around all the exposed steel parts of the cycle. I had put in a chain lock, a side stand, raised the seat and turned it at an angle. It looked like a black panther, and even the company people would not have recognized it. In a matter of a few hours, I had turned the Raleigh into a rally cycle.

Dad looked at me like I had been possessed by an evil spirit. In one glance, he took in every small change. In a strained voice, he asked me why I had destroyed the cycle. He then proceeded to point out every bit of destruction. He listed my seven deadly mistakes, each one preceded with my name, to accentuate the point. Through all this, there wasn't the faintest trace of anger, only disappointment.

1. Ananda, if the breeze is a little strong, the side stand will give way.

2. Ananda, the company's central locking is the best. Your chain lock can be opened with a hairpin.

3. Ananda, this handle facing upwards will give you *shoki* for two days. After that, you will experience severe backache.

4. Ananda, how can you not have mudguards? Your clothes will get splattered with slush.

5. Ananda, what do you have against the chain guard? It is there for a good reason. The grease will be all over your pants.

6. Ananda, mirror, I can understand. I find it useful but if you don't like it, that's wokay.

7. Ananda, and of all the things, why have you angled the seat? You will be looking somewhere and heading somewhere else. You might meet with an accident but more importantly, people will call you a fool.

Honestly, I wanted to call dad that because he just didn't get any of this. We had a little standoff, and I didn't answer. There was no way I could convince old-world logic with new-age inspiration. I realized that if I tried, I would only hurt him more. So, I looked down, looked around and generally held my ground. After a few minutes of silence,dad sighed like a tired steam engine and went inside.

· · · · · · · · · · · · · · · · · ·

(30)

HOLY VERMILLION HOLI

The academic year of 1986 was nearing its end. Our Class IX final exams were underway and the six papers were spread across 14 days. Typically, we had two sets of players:
1. Those who wanted to score in every match.
2. Those who reserved their energies for the big final.
Our first public exams were a year away and therefore I wasn't breaking a sweat. But many in school were showing symptoms of a breakdown.
It was the day of our third exam. The English paper was pretty much a nightwatchman for me. I brushed my teeth and was lazily brushing up on some topics when I suddenly realized the bigness of the day. It was Holi. Unusually this year, it had managed to squeeze into our exam schedule and that was a terrible thing. Holi was always a wonderful spectacle, but we would end up sacrificing it this year. My mind kept telling me that this shouldn't be. I decided that something had to be done. Obviously, a full-fledged Holi celebration was out of question. That would have to wait till the exams got over. But something symbolic had to happen. Given the atmosphere of final exams, buying colours and carrying them to school wasn't a good idea. Also, I realized I didn't have time. So, I started looking around the house for something colourful. Instinct took me to mom's modest dressing table that had a pint-sized box of vermillion on it. I pulled out the drawer and in the back corner was a more sizeable box, looking ignored. I didn't know if vermillion had an expiry date but if it

did, this box was at least a few years past that. Mom must have bought it at some point, put it here and clearly forgotten. I opened the box gingerly. Nothing seemed to be wrong with it except the colour. I knew what vermillion red was: bright and fiery. That was the mainstream one but it also came in a few shades. I had seen women wear a deeper, maroon shade. This one was exceptionally deep and so maroon that it was actually a dark shade of brown. It looked nothing less than muck. Time had surely sucked out its sparkle. I was excited. Mom had forgotten this box and would never notice its absence. In fact, if she did ever remember, it would be thrown out immediately. I decided to carry it to school, mix it in water and dab a few friends with it.

Soon, Giddi and I cycled to Vishak's house and our group made its way to school. It was 9:40 am, twenty minutes before the start of the exam. Hundreds of students were spread across the school ground. Some were mugging alone in the corridors, some doing group revisions and a few were startling others by throwing obscure questions. I told Giddi that we should have water before entering the examination hall. I smiled to myself as he followed me to the water taps. I wanted to dab Giddi's cheeks with the muck. He was a close friend and wouldn't complain or take offence. After the exam, I could do the same with a few others to celebrate the spirit of Holi.

A large, cement water tank with several taps, stood usefully in one corner of the school ground. It was the caravanserai to hordes of camels that attended school each day. During exams, a lot of nervous students drank water before stepping into various classrooms to face their destiny. Strangely, the tests and exams parched the throats of the most studious and the diligent ones. Walking a few steps ahead of Giddi, I stealthily pulled out the box from my pocket and tipped a handful of mud-coloured vermillion into my palm. I reached the line of taps and bent down to make it seem like I was drinking water. I gently turned the tap and collected a few drops. My palm was no container for a ploy like this. Instead of having coloured water, I had a gooey lump. Giddi by now, was to my left. Bending down, he was slurping water from his concave palm. Two taps behind Giddi, was

Praveen. He was a diminutive front-bencher, nervy and ultra-studious. He looked like a miniature camel filling himself before the two-and-a-half-hour trudge across the Empty Quarter called a question paper. As Giddi straightened up after his fill, I chucked the gooey lump at his face, from less than three feet away. Instinctively, he moved like Bruce Lee, angled his head and evaded the lump. It splotched on Praveen's right eye, covering his eyebrow and eye bag as well. He was caught totally unawares and started howling. An involuntary reflex made him cover his right eye and the goo, with an arched right palm. As the viscosity slid down, he started screaming murder. Giddi, despite being the original target had recovered from his victim's status and was now next to me, looking at Praveen's predicament. My playful spirit suddenly turned grave. Here was a near-suicidal case. We knew Praveen was the sort who would break down horribly if his Hero pen leaked a drop before a class test. But now, four minutes before the final exam, he was blind in his right eye. His left eye was also squeezed shut, maybe sympathetically. Only his mouth was ajar letting out wails. The ugly vermillion-goo held steadfastly to his eye. I jumped, took a handful of water and dislodged it. With my arm around him like a padre, I enquired with a great deal of concern.

Me: *Praveen…yen aaytho? Eega thaane seri idyallo!*

(Praveen…what happened? Just now, you were fine!)

I heard no response. Even with the lump gone, his eyes were tightly closed. I had lobbed it from such close quarters and with so much gleeful vigour that a small part of it had hit the cornea before his eyelid could impulsively shut. I gently washed it, a few times. Finally, he

managed to open his eye. It was the colour of mainstream vermillion. We were left with two minutes before the exam started, and I hurried him up the corridor with this information. Most people had vanished by now and the three of us darted up the steps to the first floor. I was out in an hour, but nervously hung around to see Praveen. At the end of the deadline, he walked out. His eye looked normal and his face, composed. Even the corners of his lips were marginally upturned. He had done well by his standards. With English and Praveen out of the way, I gathered a gang of 12-15 people. I narrated the goo incident, and we had a hearty laugh. Then, I told them that our final paper was five days away and post that, we just couldn't let Holi escape. Most of them were colourful characters and therefore, the idea of a delayed Holi held great appeal. Everyone was turned on by the thought. All of us promised to carry bags of colours on the final day, hide it in the cycle stand, rush through our paper and then have a go at each other.

The last exam was like the last batsman, totally insignificant. It was the third language paper, for a measly 50 marks. We had a phrase for it: aatakuntu lekakilla! Part of the game, with no contribution! I was so excited about playing Holi that I didn't have the patience to finish the paper. The moment I realised that I would get 30-odd marks, I walked out though I knew the answers to some of the remaining questions. One by one, the Holi gang emerged. Class IX was dead and gone. Colours and celebrations awaited us. We ran to the cycle stand and pulled out the packets. Some of us scavenged outside the main gate and found dirty glass bottles on the sides of the road. We mixed the colours and stepped onto the school premises. Smack in the middle of the central ground, we started splashing each other. Needless to add, we were running around and hollering. The exams were still on and most students were inside, either writing furiously or waiting patiently to cog in the final 15 minutes. A couple of lecturers shushed us but we paid no heed. The spirit of Holi and the added fun of playing it five days later had made us delirious. We became noisier, rowdier and started throwing colours on every schoolmate who walked out. Within 30 minutes, everyone was out, and more characters joined in. The group swelled and slowly turned riotous. With the task of the exams over, the principal and the lecturers turned their attention towards us. We were told that they would deny us admission into the 10th standard if we didn't clear the area right away. Cursing them under our breaths, we moved out. Now, we were on the main road and the merriment continued in a busy part of Shimoga. This intersection held two colleges and three other schools. Before we realized, innocuous school revelry had turned into a civil issue. We suddenly noticed two police jeeps. More constables on bikes and cycles came out of nowhere. Brandishing their lathis, they ran towards us. A few of us scrrreamed to notify everyone, to scrrram. All our adventures till now had been juvenile. This was the first time it had tipped over into serious adult land. We dashed for our lives, in any direction that beckoned us. A few tripped, pulled themselves up and managed to escape. Some jumped fences, some crashed into cycles and pedestrians, some screamed in panic while some shrieked with rebellious glee. A few unlucky ones got the end of the lathi. One got hit on the hand and had a fractured pinky. For a while, news of civil disturbance spread around the area. Alarmed students and public scurried away quickly. Thankfully, all of us managed to get away. We ran into different corners of Shimoga, far away from the scene. Hours later, we regrouped in different sets and towards the evening, cautiously came back to collect our cycles.

In a matter of five days, from a vermillion-goo to a lathi charge, we had lost a part of our innocence.

. . . .

(31

THIRD LANGUAGE

They had left home after breakfast. At 11 am, they entered the forest and now it was nearly teatime. But they hadn't had lunch, or even water in hours.

Lord Rama, Lakshmana and Sita continued walking deeper into the forest. They had just started their vanavas and had years to go. They walked to the sound of birds overhead. Deers kept jumping here and there. Lakshmana was walking ahead looking out for any potential danger. At the same time, he was also looking for food, water and shelter. Lord Rama and Sita were a few paces behind him, discussing their family problems. Suddenly, Lakshmana froze. He sensed someone behind one of the trees. Unsure whether it was a *mitra* or a *shatru*, he immediately pulled out his bow and arrow. As he readied himself, he saw that the man behind the tree already had his arrow pointed at him. Next to him was a person who looked bigger than Dara Singh. This built-like-a-bully-and-a-bulldozer man was carrying a mace. Lakshmana wanted to run back, but by then Lord Rama and Sita were next to him. Rama held up his benign palm, smiled and asked the two strangers,
Lord Rama: *Please introduce your good selves.*
Smaller Guy: *Arjuna.*
Big Guy: *Bheema!*

Rama, Lakshmana and Sita smiled. These two didn't sound like *rakshasas*. In fact, they also looked like they had been driven away from Home, and were wandering aimlessly in the forest. Now, the three of them introduced themselves and the other two smiled in comfort. Both parties felt that they were dealing with good men. It was clear to Lakshmana that the other two had been in the forest longer, and so he enquired,

Lakshmana: *Arjuna, where can we find some cold water?*

Bheema immediately pulled out a pot of water from behind the tree. Rama, Lakshmana and Sita had never tasted water that was as sweet, cold and refreshing as this. As they emptied the pot, Arjuna asked them, smiling with great knowledge,

Arjuna: *Isn't it better than `Rephrigerator' water?*

The three couldn't agree with him more and nodded robustly.

That's when I woke up. It was easily the most bizarre dream that I had ever had. If I was younger, I probably would have been disoriented but being in the eighth standard, I realized that most dreams were like dustbins; everything got totally mixed up. One thing in particular amused me no end - `Rephrigerator'.

I was now in high school, and we had to study a third language. My mind always looked to the future because I knew I wouldn't spend my whole life in Shimoga. So, any foreign language would come handy at some point. Instead, I had to travel thousands of years back in time and learn Sanskrit. I didn't understand its use or purpose. Also, I didn't get the grammar and the pronunciation. In fact, the only people in the world who spoke in Sanskrit lived just ten kilometres outside of Shimoga, in a village called Mattur. I don't know why they still spoke this archaic language. Maybe, they didn't want anybody in the world to understand them. Our Sanskrit teacher called HSS came from this village. Most teachers were known by their initials: HMP, BSA, HRK, KRS etc. When expanded, HSS could have possibly been Hayagreeva Shankaranarayana Sashwathachar. So, none of us even ventured there and stuck to his initials. He was a good teacher and had his brand of humour, but to me, the subject he taught was neither good nor fun.

Ramam, Ramau, Ramaha…
Aham, Aavam, Vayam, Twayam…
Idam, Kadapi, Kintu, Sahaja…
Dridha, Kshipta, Laghu, Sakhi, twam…
and more nonsense…and I don't understand a thing… and I am not interested… and I will stop now!

I had gone into severe *atma vichara* (self-enquiry) about why I had to learn this language. Self-enquiry never gives immediate answers and so, I had to go through it for three years. But immediately, I wanted something that could hold my attention in class. HSS had two peculiarities. On the very first day, he had asked all of us to introduce ourselves. He wanted to know our names and the names of our native places. For the next three years, he addressed each of us by the name of the place we came from.

HSS: *Ye Thirthalli! Ye Harnalli! Ye Mandarti! Ye Koppa! Ye Honnali! Ye Sirsi! Ye Kumsi! Ye Hosalli!*

These were all names of small towns and villages around Shimoga. *Ye* was short for yelling out for the student. This was quite insane. He just looked at a student and correctly addressed him or her, by the name of the town. In three years, he never once got it wrong. He could have done better in life if he'd been in the postal department. His other peculiarity was his use of English. The Sanskrit textbook had excess Ramayana and Mahabharata and to HSS, this was the ultimate era to live in. According to him, everything in that era was *sagkhyatita* (innumerable) times better than our present world. And he always made it a point to run down the world we lived in. Each time he did that, he used an English word in the context of our current times. The previous day, he had used 'Rephrigerator'. The entire class had burst out laughing. In the profundity of Ramayana and Mahabharatha in Sanskrit, the English words stood out like *maanikyams* (gems). If a modern English term in the midst of archaic Sanskrit wasn't funny enough, he upped the humour quotient with his pronunciation. This wasn't deliberate though. He put an 'h' in every English word, either because of speaking Sanskrit or because his name started with an 'h'.

When I reached school, I told the gang about my drheam. We laughed like *yuyukkhuras* (hyenas). The Sanskrit problem was solved in my head. Since that day, I managed to start paying attention in his class, looking forward to the next English word that popped out of his mouth. Of course, my mind only sought them out and nothing in between. Everyone around me – Vishak, Deepak, Pandu, Simmu, Shashi Kiran – started doing the same. Soon, our books were littered with HSS's English words. Every time he used one in the course of a lesson, we scribbled it down in the textbook. A few months later, a bunch of us ranked, argued over the list, and finally made an anthology.

HSS PLATINUM HITS (No.5)
In the context of Pushpaka Vimana,
HSS: *Idhru mundhe Yuh Yheff Foh yenu illa!*
(UFO is nothing in front of this!)

HSS PLATINUM HITS (No.4)
While describing a woman in some epic,
HSS: *Pakwabimbadharóshthi!*
(Her lips were the color of a morning reddish sun.)
HSS: *Without using any red lipistick [sic]*

HSS PLATINUM HITS (No.3)
When talking about Hanumantha and Sanjeevani,
HSS: *Aa kaaladalli dihseases kintha mehdicines jaasti ithu!*
(In that era, they had more medicines than diseases!)

HSS PLATINUM HITS (No.2)
When Maricha turned himself into a golden deer and aided Ravana in kidnapping Sita,
HSS: *Ghender change yenu, sphecies change-ye maadkond bidthidru!*
(Forget gender change, they even managed species change!)

HSS PLATINUM HITS (No.1)
HSS: *Aa yeradu bettagalu bhreasts tarah kandanu.*

(He beheld those two hills as breasts.)

He was teaching Meghadootha and someone in that great lyrical poem, had seen the hills as described above, while flying over them. Of course, it was Kalidasa's imagination and HSS's explanation.

HSS: *Ee kaaladalli imhaginationu illa, bhreastsu illa!*

(In this era, there's neither imagination nor breasts!)

HSS was a most straightforward man and didn't mean anything apart from the fact that everything was awesome in that era. But in the back benches of the class, I remember most of us tittering and whispering various names that contradicted his argument. Anyway, this list of English words grew every day and so did our glee and involvement. Whenever I opened the Sanskrit textbook at home to study, I only looked at all the scribbled words, guffawed and shut it. After months of this crazy life, I was now sitting breathless and clueless. I was staring at the Sanskrit examination paper: *Kumarasambhava, Dandakaranya,* some verb forms, *Abhignanashakuntalam, Malavikagnimitram,* some grammar nonsense, *Raghuvamsa, Rutusamhara…*

One glance at the question paper and I had given up. Nothing made sense. I had been a good student for the most part and finally, here was this third language paper threatening me with utter failure. In this stressed-out state, English words kept dancing around in my head. At one point, I thought I will simply write down: *I prefer Sita's agnipareeksha to this yheggzamination paper!*

After calming myself, I looked around for help like Lord Rama had done, before going to Lanka. Arvind, seated in the bench ahead, became my Hanumantha. He shiftily showed me his answer sheet and thereby the way to cross over to the ninth standard. Over the next one hour, I kept peering into this benefactor's sheet and managed a first class in the third language.

. . . .

(32)

THREE FOURTH PANTS

Clothes maketh the man. This is the deeper part of the saying. The simpler part is: man maketh the clothes. There can't be a bigger testimony to this than what took place in 1987.

Mom had a sewing machine and operated it like a semi-professional. She used it for altering blouses, hemming trouser bottoms, stitching falls for sarees, adjusting waist sizes and other tasks. Watching her, I had picked up the art of doing some sewing. I couldn't handle the waist but anything below it was well within my means. On some Sundays, I would pull out a pant handed down to me, and alter its length. It happened to be one of those sewing Sundays. Mom had gone to visit a friend, dad was on duty and Sriram was out. I was in the mood to do something either exciting or constructive. I opened the cupboard and suddenly remembered a pair of trousers that had come down to me from my cousin in Madras. Ramesh was six years older and had his own sense of style. It was a polyester pair in a shade of grey. Each leg was wide enough to accommodate a mango tree trunk. I liked the colour but would have to alter it significantly. As I was sizing it up, Giddi walked in.

Giddi: *Carrom aadona?*

(Shall we play carrom?)

Me: *Volle Sunday. Mood yaake haal maadkothya?*

(Why do you want to ruin your mood on a glorious Sunday?)

To be fair, Giddi was an equally good player. We both had our individual styles and his winning percentage was close to mine. Giddi looked at the pant dangling from my hand.

Giddi: *Yeno Dabba? Ee pantige elephantiasis aag hogide!*

(What Dabba? This pant is suffering from elephantiasis!)

Me: *Correctu. Camelitis maadi, length-alli Dabbaitis maad beku.)*

(Correct. Have to turn this to camelitis and in length, Dabbaitis.)

He chortled, took the trousers from me and stretched it on the floor. With the inch tape, I measured the length and marked the point where I had to snip them. Through this, we were tripping on our `animals & diseases' wordplay and kept laughing. I picked up the pair of scissors, asked Giddi to hold the pant stretched and snipped off both legs. When I held it up at my waist, I couldn't believe my eyes. In the first and only instance of such an oversight, I had snipped it way too short. It stood two inches below my knee. Giddi was also aghast as he had seen me alter clothes before. I kept staring at this neither-here-nor-there vestment. Giddi carried on with his rubbish wordplay.

Giddi: *Shrinkitis! Monkeyitis!*

I found it intriguing, declared it awesome and told Giddi that this would be the new trend. Giddi had to shove his fist into his mouth to control his merriment.

Giddi: *Simple! Swalpa chop maadu. Bombaat shorts aag hogathe.*

(Simple! Chop off a bit and you have a fabulous pair of shorts.)

In my head, chopping it further was easy and boring. Here was something that had happened by chance, and none of us had ever seen anything like this. I thought the length was groovy. I was capricious at times, but this was pushing the boundaries. I hemmed the bottom of the trousers, altered the width, wore them and walked around the house. We didn't have a full-length mirror and so I relied on Giddi's feedback. He shook his head several times and left for home, shaking it all the way. I was excited and couldn't wait for Monday to dawn.

When mom came back, I proudly displayed it to her. She didn't take it seriously and remarked that I looked like a scavenger. The next morning, I was getting ready for school. Our uniform was, white shirt and grey bottoms. We were in high school and the authorities weren't too strict about the shades. My 3/4ths more than qualified. Dad was sitting with the Deccan Herald, but he couldn't take his eyes off me. To him, even a pair of jeans was anathema. He felt it didn't behoove our upbringing. His sartorial righteousness was made up of cotton and terylene.

Dad: *Please change. Cun-ser-ven-see aur tarah dress maadkond idhiya.*

(Please change. You are dressed like conservancy people.)

This was one of the words the Britishers had left behind, and people in the railway quarters used it generously. The railways had Grade V employees called scavengers who belonged to the conservancy department. They were often seen about clearing rot, cleaning gutters and toilets, with their pants folded up. I looked at dad who looked like he was having a cardiac arrest. I pulled up my socks and put on my pair of sneakers. I jumped on my bicycle and went to Vishak's house. Deepak Shetty and Amogha were already waiting. The three of them looked at me incredulously.

Deepak: *Dabba, yeno idhu?*

(What the hell is this!)

Me: *Idhe stylu. Bombaat, alva?*

(This is the style. Fabulous, no?)

They didn't know what to do. They just stood there utterly shocked and embarrassed and didn't want to be seen with me.

Vishak: *Aiyo! Yoondhu sahawasane beda!*

(Oh God! I wish I wasn't in his company!)

I rallied them to start cycling as we were running late for school. We rode into the school bicycle stand. The mayhem began. As we walked from the cycle stand to our classroom, hundreds of students walked behind me. It was clearly my Dandi March moment, except that most of them stared disjointedly at my legs. Inside the class, everyone went, `WHAT THE ....?'. The blank space had a choice of a hundred expressions through the day, including a lot of blanks. No one knew what to say or how to react. Some rolled their eyes in wonder, some stayed agape through the day, some touched it, and a few forgot their own names. By late afternoon, a handful had managed to form some coherent questions and comments around it.

Shashikiran: *Where have you seen this?*

Pandu: *With parents like yours, why are you so crazy?*

PP Anand: *You can turn them into shorts, no?*

PP Anand was one of the frontbenchers and a bookworm. His mind was so organized that it thought only in straight lines. If you asked him, `Which came first, the chicken or the egg?', he was most likely to respond thus: *Arun Sharma came first, Narasimha came second, and I came sixth in our mid-term exam.*

I told PP that I had years more of growth and slowly but surely, this would turn into a pair of shorts on its own; that I had decided to let it take its natural course. He scratched his head and went back to his textbook. By the end of the day, the accidental pants had become the talk of the town. DVS High School aside, students in many schools and colleges around were only discussing this. As our gang cycled back home, various people stood along the way for a glimpse. We felt stares of admiration and annoyance. Quite a few senior students were miffed and called me names, very risible ones. I realized that creating news was also a matter of seniority. The juniors weren't supposed to. Everyone in my group begged me to either get rid of them or ride alone. I discarded both suggestions. This initial brouhaha lasted a week and slowly Shimoga learnt to live with it. I wore this amazing pair every third day. Discussions and comments continued to crop up every now and then but by and large, it had nestled its way into our society. Dad remained where he was. Every morning, as I got ready to leave for school, he would mutter in a resigned tone,

Dad: *Huchchan tarah kaanthya!*

(You look like an imbecile!)

At the end of the year, we had our Social Day. I was the school leader and had to be on the podium along with the principal, the chief guest and a few lecturers. You need not guess what I wore that day.

· · · · · · ·· · ·· · ·· · · · ·· · ·

_(33)_

AZHAR

We were in Class IX, a gang of tight-knit, happy friends. Studies and cricket filled up most of our days, but we were constantly seeking out newer experiences. The year was 1986 but, in a sense, this was our Orwellian 1984. We discovered something that gave us a different view of the world. While flipping through a magazine called Mirror, we came across Pen Pals. Till then, we had never heard of this concept. One day, it just reached out from a magazine page and pulled us right in. Strangely, only Vishak and I were bitten by the bug. The rest of the gang gave this a pass. Deepak Shetty was content with his SportStars, SportsWeeks and SportsWorlds. Amogha had taken up badminton seriously and was pushing into the state rankings. Narasimha had his hands full with trigonometry, Sanskrit, burettes and pipettes, taxonomy, Euclid's geometry and gravity. We were a year away from the all-important public exams, but he had started his sprint already. One non-academic pursuit he allowed himself, was cricket. He would join the gang precisely for 47 minutes every evening. He needed 13 minutes to cycle back home, wash his hands and feet, and open his textbooks.

Vishak and I, however, were immediately taken in. To us, the concept of Pen Pals was magical. You could write to anyone, anywhere in the world, share your life and get to know his or hers. We started sending out dozens of letters. I wasn't sure if mom and dad would take kindly to strangers sending me letters, and so used Vishak's address. We wrote to people in Kohima and Bangalore, Norway, Dhaka and other exotic places. We made contact with people of our age, and some, older than our parents. We used postcards, inland letters and Air Mail. Niju's dad worked in the post office, and we got our supplies easily without having to stand in a queue for long. We enquired about their life, climate and games, food habits, holiday destinations, favourite authors, movies and sports personalities. We exchanged poems, stamps and exotic leaves. Shimoga had some unique plants, just like their places did. By now, we were familiar with botany and could handpick some pretty interesting species of local flora. We invited some of them to visit us. We could easily host them in Vishak's house. A few made plans and subsequently cancelled, because just like us, they had their exams going on. During their holidays, they had their aunts and uncles to visit, just as we did. In that year, and maybe for a while after, till we lost interest and contact, we could have visited forty-three towns in five countries. Soon, Vishak and I had a little one-upmanship game going on between us. We were very thick and so, marks, money and material things held no significance. It was the number of Pen Pals and each successive letter one got that drove the other to do better. Once or twice, we took out our atlases, dotted the world map with our contacts and compared. We had some very interesting patterns and were running close to each other. After a few months of doing this, the excitement started waning. People wrote back with either too much, or too little. Most didn't have the sense to engage the reader. They wrote about their families and favourite cousins, best friends, waterfalls, Christmas lunch, and basically about a lot of things that had no relevance to us. Some wrote back saying that they were fine and asking us if we were doing fine. I was pretty sure those letter writers would do badly in their exams. We had started out with two-page letters that soon came down to two paragraphs. Initially, we responded within two days, which then started getting stretched to beyond a week. After a gap of 8-9 days, it became very difficult to dig into the past and respond from the heart. It slowly dawned on us that long-distance friendships don't work. On a Sunday, we decided to put an end to this mindless exercise. We wrote a crisp letter stating that our parents didn't approve of this friendship. We gave it credence by stating that Shimoga was a small town, and most people had even smaller mindsets, starting with our parents. We then copied this letter several times and sent it to all our Pen Pals. The letters dried up.

This was a relief, and we were now free to do more significant things. Vishak and I decided to become Pen Pals with the high and the mighty. This would be worth every paragraph and every paisa. And so, we made our wish list. Some of the personalities who figured prominently in my list were Mikhail Gorbachev, Rajiv Gandhi, Jackie Chan, Michael Jackson, Joel Garner, Amitabh Bachchan and Kareem Abdul Jabbar. Vishak had his own set of names, and Gorbachev figured in both lists. But Vishak was also crazy about Azharuddin. In his books, Azhar could do no wrong, and thankfully for Vishak, Azhar was phenomenal in almost every match he played then. Vishak himself was the poorest man's version of Azhar. He had picked up all the mannerisms but not an iota of skill. He used to claim that he had the best wrists in our team, but no runs used to come off them. He was a pathetic fielder and a disastrous runner between the wickets. But he felt he had the spirit of Azhar in him, and that it would shine forth someday. Obviously, he sent a letter to Azhar. I sent an Air Mail to the Kremlin, and also wrote to Rajiv Gandhi. After a brief background about Shimoga and myself, I put down a list of questions, on a variety of issues:

1. Which school and college did you go to?
2. What were your favourite subjects?
3. Were you ever made to kneel down in class?
4. Could you please send me a signed photograph of yours?
5. Do you eat only chapatis or also eat rice?
6. How was the recent SAARC Summit?

The last two questions deserve special mention. As a kid, I had frequently heard people say that North Indians eat only chapatis. I could never imagine life without rice, and this had played on my mind while growing up. On several occasions, I had thanked God for putting me in rice country and not up there. Obviously, by now, I had the wisdom to conjecture that this wasn't entirely true. But I realized that I wouldn't be writing to the Prime Minister frequently, and hence decided to settle this once and for all. To compensate for this inanity, I threw in the last question. The SAARC Summit had just gotten over and had received more-than-necessary-coverage in the national and local media. It bored me and I had no stomach for more information. But my instinct said that, if anything at all, this might get me a response.

After having sent our respective letters, Vishak and I would come home from school every day, and the first thing would be to ask our moms about any letters. Days passed and none turned up. We were utterly disappointed and realized that we had aimed too high. Obviously, all of them were world personalities and had too much on their plates to respond to us. We gave up hope, slowly. A few weeks later, I reached home from school. Mom looked at me strangely and asked if I had written to the Indian Government. I twisted my face in confusion, and suddenly let out a scream of delight. This was December 6, 1986. Along with my cup of tea, she handed me a packet. Shaking with excitement, I opened it and saw a booklet on Rajiv Gandhi. It spoke about his growing up years, entry into politics, achievements, legacy and vision for the country. There was no signed photograph though. But there was a letter sent on his behalf by Smt. Rajeshwari Tandon, his Social Secretary.

To be honest, I was a little disappointed, but still, the fact that I had received a response, thrilled me no end. This was surely a first for the railway quarters if not, Shimoga. Even mom was quite impressed. I skipped my evening tiffin and ran to Vishak's house with the packet. The gang obviously went nuts. The next day, when dad came home from his train duty, I showed it to him. He complimented me but also added that both the PMO and I should be focusing on our jobs, instead of exchanging letters.

F. NO. 7 (16) 86 - PM IV

Smt. Rajeshwari Tandon
Social Sedretary to PM

प्रधान मंत्री कार्यालय
नई दिल्ली 110 011
PRIME MINISTER'S OFFICE
NEW DELHI 110 011

November 25, 1986

1 DEC 1986

Dear Anand,

 The Prime Minister has received your letter of November 8 and has asked me to reply on his behalf owing to his many preoccupations at this time.

 I enclose a biographical sketch which answers the questions you have asked.

 The recent SAARC Conference was an effort to find new ideas and impulses that will strengthen bonds, and to bring the neighbouring countries of South Asia together. It has been generally felt that a new political thrust needs to be given to the growing economic activities of the this developing region of the world. There was also a SAARC Conference on children concerning health, nutrition and education programmes for the young people of South Asia.

 The Prime Minister has conveyed his good wishes for your studies and for a bright future.

     Yours sincerely,

     (Rajeshwari Tandon)

Master S. Anand
S/o Sh. N. Subba Rao
116/A Railway Quarters
Shimoga - 577201
KARNATAKA

After this, I was hopeful of getting a letter from Moscow, but it never turned up.

Sometime in January, I went to Bangalore for three days, to attend a family function at my aunt's place, in Malleswaram. Two days after my return, all of us, as usual, were at Vishak's house, after school. Narasimha, Deepak, Niju, Giddi and a couple of others were on the terrace, ready to begin our short tennis. Cricket was our staple game but short tennis had taken over our lives, at this point in time. Like short cricket, we had a version of tennis that we played with our palms. This wasn't for time pass though. When you are in the ninth standard, you don't play to while away time, but to set records and humiliate your opponents. We had just one surface (the terrace), but we had allocated different days to different Grand Slams. Following the legacy of the Slams, we would also play a serve-and-volley or a baseline game. Some days, we turned the cart on our opponents and played a net game during our French Open. The net was a two-feet wide, three-feet high concrete slab that ran across the terrace. We played Singles and Doubles, and had all the drama that went on in the real circuit: tough draws, bad line calls, injuries, sledging, last-minute pullouts etc.

On this particular day, Vishak came up five minutes late, and called out my name. Both his hands were behind his back, and he had an expression that reminded me of Jesse Owens in 1936. I asked him to be out with whatever it was. Without saying a word, he preened and extended a letter to me.

Me: *Bhukali?*

(Hope you are not kidding?)

Everyone gathered in a tight circle as I unfolded it.

January 18, 1986

Dear Vishak,

Thank you for your letter.
I am so happy to know that you are such a big fan of mine.

I am sorry for replying late as I was travelling.
At your age, I was also just like you, playing my natural game and enjoying cricket. Thanks to Allah, I now play for India. I hope and pray that you also play for the country one day.
You've told me that you are strong on the leg-side. That's good, but I will advise you to practise your off-side strokes.
The other important thing is fielding. Spend time working on it. As you know, catches win matches, and you have to take every single catch.

Best wishes and hope to see you in the team soon.

Sincerely
Mohd. Azharuddin

All of us read the letter again and again, and screamed each time. We hugged and congratulated Vishak. He couldn't control his joy and did a little dance. He was slightly ungainly and would never do anything like this, unless it was something truly special.

After all of us settled down and were about to start our game of tennis, I called out to him in the very same casual tone he'd called out to me. I told him that the letter was a fake. There was silence like we had never heard before. Everyone searched my face. Vishak was so shaken that he stood absolutely still. He then pooh-poohed my claim, laughing it off. I waited for Vishak's laughter to subside, and then repeated, `That letter is a fake!'. This time, the reactions were more tense and irritated. I had got on their nerves. Vishak looked agitated and said that I was talking rubbish because I was jealous. I informed everyone that he had handed over only the letter to me, and not the envelope. That had been with him throughout and I hadn't seen it. I asked him where this letter should have come from. Vishak thought for a moment before saying, Hyderabad. I told him that this letter was from Bangalore, and asked him to check the stamping around the stamp. I hadn't seen the envelope and couldn't be so sure if I didn't know its origin. Five faces stared at me as if I was either a genius, or a monster. As Vishak slowly pulled out the envelope from his pocket, I also added that the stamping would say Malleswaram Post Office. I had been to Bangalore a few days earlier, and the family function had been at my aunt's house in Malleswaram.

The stamp on the envelope backed me up. I had never seen Vishak look and feel more miserable. He retreated into a corner of his big terrace. He didn't speak for the next hour and a half. Everyone else was truly mad at me. They told me that I had gone way too far with this gag. I insisted that it had been an impulsive prank, and that they were making a waterfall out of a teardrop. That evening, the French Open was called off.

Vishak was a person with a lot of heart. Being the darling that he was, he managed to gather himself by the end of the evening. As we left his house at seven, he smiled weakly and told me that he would never forget this. I apologized profusely and said, `*Neither will I!*'.

(34)

FLOOD OF MEMORIES

I was back from Calcutta. Sitting with the gang, I was narrating
the trip in all its colourful details.
Giddi: *Bhukali beda!*
(Don't make it up!)
I pinched the skin on my throat.
Me: *Devraane!*
(God promise!)
I admitted that I had a knack of making up tall tales, but never the
intent. I added that memories have the nasty habit of garnishing
what really happened, but in this specific case, it turned out
exactly the way I had shared it.
Every year, the Indian Railways conducted trips for kids of
railway employees. It was a state-wise programme. The Northern
Railways took children to West or South India; Southern Railways
organized a trip to the East or the North, and so on. It was a part of
a welfare scheme where the children of railway employees got to
see their country at highly subsidized prices. The year was 1988
and Karnataka announced its railway trip. For a sum of
seventy-five rupees, they offered an 11-day excursion: 3 days of
sightseeing in Calcutta, a 2-day halt at Bhubhaneshwar on the
way back, with trips to Jagannath Puri, Chandrabhaga beach and
Konark Sun Temple. It was quite a marvel the way they ran it.
Group: An upper limit of fifty, including girls. It comprised
children from various cities and towns from across the state, based

on a quota system. Bangalore, being the capital, had the biggest quota of 15 children. This was followed by Mysore, which could send in 8 kids. Similarly, depending on the size, each town got its share. Arasikere got 3, Birur got 2, while towns like Shimoga, Bhadravati and Talguppa got one each. The Station Master put up the circular and interested employees submitted the names of their wards. Children between the ages of 5 and 15 were eligible.

Entourage: To take care of 50 disparate kids, 6 railway employees (guards, an asst. stationmaster, TTEs) were chosen and appointed as tour officials. To feed this jamboree of 56 people, 2 cooks were picked to be a part of the journey. On this trip, both were from the Mysore railway canteen.

Journey: Since this was a subsidized trip, the railways had a rule for the excursion bogie. It could only be attached to passenger mails, not to an express train. Against the norm of the guard compartment being the last car, this bogie got attached behind it. It would go up to whichever point the passenger mail went, in the general direction towards Calcutta. At a particular station, if the passenger mail had to end its journey or veer off, the bogie got detached, shunted and placed on a subsidiary track. It would then wait for the next passenger mail heading in the general direction towards Calcutta. So, when the journey finally began, we took three and a half days to reach Howrah Junction from Bangalore.

Food: Being a highly discounted trip, the railways couldn't afford to buy food from outside. Of course, when we went sightseeing, they would buy modest lunch packets. Otherwise, most of the time was spent on the train. Breakfast, lunch and dinner would be cooked for 58 people on a running train. This part was the most incredible thing. A bogie has 4 toilets, one each at the extreme ends, and two in the middle. One toilet at the end was sealed and turned into a storeroom. It was stacked with sacks of rice, dal, potatoes, onions, packets of condiments, curry leaves, tamarind, red and green chillies, cans of kerosene, cooking oil, utensils etc. Along the journey, the cooks would replenish things as and when needed. Just outside the toilet was a long, 2-burner stove. In the corner on the left was a big IndianOil tar drum. This was a virgin drum and yet, had been scrubbed endlessly to make it sambar-worthy. They would cook sambar in two big vessels at a time, but to feed 58 people, they would have to do at least two rounds. They would store the sambar in the drum and serve people from it. About 70% of the tar drum was enough to feed the group. Rice and sabzi would be served out of large aluminium buckets.

Sleeping Arrangements: An entire 2-tier sleeper coach was reserved for the group. This bogie had uncushioned, wooden sleepers. Each compartment had upper and lower berths and across the aisle, two lower wooden seats and a berth above. The two lower wooden seats could be turned into a berth by stacking suitcases in between, which is what I finally did when the trip began (I'll explain the logic of this when we get there.) If you counted all the berths and the seats-converted- to-berths in the entire bogie, they added up to 55, a deficit of 3.

Bathing: Every morning, the train usually reached a junction and stopped for about half an hour, or more. Here, the senior staff would get off and hasten to the Waiting Room, which usually had a couple of bathrooms. After speaking to the railway authorities and making arrangements, they would lead the girls and wait outside while the girls bathed and freshened up. Each girl got no more than five minutes. Then, they would bathe quickly and head back. The boys, because of their numbers, didn't get this privilege. They had to bathe in the open, between two sets of railway tracks. The large water pipes, used for filling bogies, poured out more than 30 mugs of water a second. The boys would crowd around two such pipes, take turns and bathe quickly. This was the quick part. The quick and dirty part was, washing underwear. We were instructed to carry detergent bars and clothesline pegs. The entire group, fresh and glowing, would be back in the bogie, ten minutes before departure. The towels would be put to dry inside the bogie while the underwear went on the window bars. Being the peak of Summer, they dried within an hour and went inside kit bags and suitcases. After every such stop, when the train finally departed, the last bogie would carry a spectacular sight for people outside the train: bystanders on the platform, people waiting at railway crossings, those working in fields etc. At the end of a long train would be a bogie with an underwear-rainbow on the window bars. Unfortunately for me, I was always on the wrong side of this, unable to take in what was without doubt, a remarkable view.

General Instructions: Apart from clothes, personal toiletries and pocket money, all of us had to carry a steel plate, spoon and tumbler. When food was ready to be served, the cook would jangle a steel ladle against a steel plate, to cue to the entire coach to fish out their crockery.

A few weeks earlier, I didn't even know the existence of this trip. I had just finished my tenth standard final exams. Two months would go by in games, schemes and a trip to Bangalore to visit my aunt. Dad came home from work one day and told me about it. He asked me if I would be interested. He did add that since I had just crossed 15 years of age, I wasn't technically eligible but that he could swing it. My eyes rolled with interest, at the opportunity to see far-flung lands and meet interesting people from different parts of my own state. I begged dad to try everything in his capacity to get me through. Two days later, dad had worked his magic and said that we would depart from Bangalore on May 8, 1988. The trip would start and end in Bangalore, and kids from other places had to make their way here and back. At 6 pm, dad and I walked down platform 4 of Bangalore railway station. I was so excited that I felt butterflies in my head, a feeling much preferable to having them in the stomach. As we closed in on the group, something seemed terribly wrong to me. I saw a long line of kids with their cheap suitcases and kit bags. In my version, I had fantasized about most of them being of my age with a generous sprinkling of natty girls. This group resembled a line at a Midday Meal Scheme. The average age of the group was eight. It had 6 girls, the oldest of whom was nine. There were three more kids around 10 years of age, and the rest were all so small that they could easily slide down a train toilet drain. The youngest was five years and a few months. There was just one other teen, from Mysore, who was 14 years, a year younger to me. I couldn't fathom how parents had let such young pups go on such a long journey with absolute strangers, the security of the railways notwithstanding. A few of them addressed me as `uncle'. The whole thing was a shocker, but this wasn't all. Most kids were from the railway schools. Some of them had even donned their uniform made from a coarse dark blue cloth. Everything in these schools were discounted and disregarded: textbooks, uniforms, meals, aptitude. A lot of employees admitted their children to these schools, either due to genuine inadequacy or a simple lack of desire to improve their lot. In most cases, this signalled the end, right at the beginning. Most kids studied for a few years, bummed around and aspired for a railway posting as firemen, linesmen or loco shed workers. I am sure there were exceptions though. Certain parents (mine included) tried their best to keep their children away from the railways. They stretched their incomes and somehow put their kids in a private school, preferably a convent. Butterflies turned into breathlessness. 14 days with this bunch? No way! Who would I talk to? What would we talk about? This was tantamount to having broad gauge and narrow gauge sit next to each other. I desperately wanted to back out but didn't know what to tell dad. He would throw a fit. At times like these, the worst thoughts crept into my head, and I seriously prayed for a stroke or some bigger misfortune.

Dad was happily chatting with some of the staff and parents. From his expression, I figured that he was making genial enquiries about the logistics of the trip. The bogie doors opened. The staff instructed us to form a straight line in the descending order of age. I didn't get the wisdom of this rule but it surely worked to my benefit. I was heading the queue and the 14-year-old from Mysore stood behind me. The staff had the first choice of seats and all of them chose upper berths. As I was the next oldest, I had my say. This was May and the height of Summer. We were heading to a part of India that was many notches hotter than Karnataka. Keeping this in mind, I chose the two wooden seats across the aisle as this gave me access to two windows. I had my hard Safari suitcase. I borrowed two more, stacked them in the middle and had a makeshift berth. The rest of the crowd selected their berths and settled in. The last three boys didn't get a berth or a seat. This wasn't meant to be but there had been some miscalculation of either the group or the berths. So, in the middle of the bogie, beside the central toilets, these three kids put down their kit bags and made little rectangles with folded bedsheets. This was on the floor and would be their beds for the rest of the trip. The days would be spent hopping around but come nightfall, and these three would have to retire here.

It was twenty minutes to departure. Parents started doing what parents always do: buying glucose biscuits and bananas. Soon the goodbyes happened and the train slowly inched out of the platform. It was 7:10 pm. Inside, the bogie was funereal. Firstly, most of the kids were young and away from home with strangers from different places. Some were depressed, some homesick, some overwhelmed and a few, shell-shocked. Everyone was in his or her designated place staring out of the window, thinking of home, parents and friends. I was staring out of two windows cursing myself for jumping at this trip. I could've had such a blast in Shimoga with my friends, but here I was heading into 11 days of gloom. One kid was playing a game on his Casio watch, some had dozed off, and not a word was spoken. Everyone was stuck in a thought-junction as an hour went by. The train had crossed over to Andhra. The sudden jangle of the ladle against the steel plate stirred most of us. The first dinner on a running train had been announced. It was 8:35 pm. The cooks had been at it from the minute we were on board. The bogie crackled to life. There were sounds of zipper bags opening, and metallic noises as plates, spoons and tumblers tumbled out. I fished out my set and vacantly stared at the two cooks who had started serving, from one end of the train. From where I was, I just had to tilt my head to the left to see the pantry side. One cook was serving rice from a bucket. The other had the IndianOil tar drum in front of him. After serving one compartment, he would push the drum a couple of feet ahead and start serving the next.

This is the moment that should be chronicled in the history of Southern Railways. The train suddenly shook like trains often do: *gaddad-raddad-gaddad-raddad-gadadadadadadad...da...da...da.* The cook lost his balance momentarily, leaned on the tar drum in front of him and without meaning to, pushed it down. I didn't catch the precise moment when the drum hit the deck. I only saw a flood of sambar gushing down the aisle. Within a minute, a large part of the bogie carried a centimetre of sambar all around. Kids started yelling and wailing. Some had managed to get their feet up in the nick of time but in the ensuing mayhem, many other feet had accidentally come down. The three kids on the floor yowled and were standing up as vertical displays of sambar. The staff, all of whom were on the upper berths, were shouting orders, which no one heard or followed. Sambar had seeped into kit bags, suitcases and every pore of those three kids. It was a messy ruin, to say the least.

Everyone was motionless for five minutes till the train pulled into the next station. It was a small, one-horse Andhra town that stood worthlessly in the midst of nothing. It was in darkness except for a small light outside the Station Master's cabin. His cabin was the only structure and he, the only living thing around. The platform couldn't have been longer than a couple of bogies. Our bogie was promptly detached. The passenger mail whistled a cheery goodbye and carried on. Thirty-seven tainted kids lined up on the platform with their suitcases and kit bags. A huge railway hose came out from between the tracks. The staff held this python and sprayed us. Thankfully, it was May and we were in Andhra, to boot. We wanted more of this water cannon. Most of the clothes were pulled out of the bags and given a spray as well. They were then laid out on the platform. The clothes and the bags dried up in a couple of hours. Meanwhile, the cooks had ignited their kerosene stove on the platform and started boiling dal again. One *gadadadadadadadad* had managed to throw the group dynamics in the opposite direction. There was much laughter, taunting and camaraderie. Dinner was ready close to midnight, and 58 of us had a feast.

From here on, it was a memorable train journey. We reached Calcutta on the fourth day. Our bogie was promptly shunted and placed on the sixth track, close to the loco shed. We spent the day resting in the bogie. A few staff members went out to organize a bus for sightseeing the next day. The rest of us sang songs, applied toothpaste to various parts of a sleeping kid and indulged in more madness. The next morning, we were up early and ready by eight. The cooks had been up earlier and were ready with upma. I ate my share. While the group was getting ready, I ambled down and saw the loco shed canteen. They were selling a plate of puri-aloo for 25 paise. They called these *luchis*. I picked up a plate and the next instant, seven kids from my group crowded around me, the uncle, begging me to buy them a plate each. Dad had given me seventy rupees for the trip along with severe instructions not to spend it on random things. This was a huge amount because everything was taken care of. He had told me repeatedly that this was `just in case' money. I sponsored luchis for all of them, not just that day but over the next two as well. We went sightseeing, marvelled at some things, didn't think much of the crowds, walked on Howrah Bridge, crossed the Hoogly in a ferry, sweated worse than pigs, rode the tram and the metro, saw Nehru Planetarium, insisted that we either ride the metro or sit in the Planetarium, because everything else was too sweaty, drove around Salt Lake, had packet lunch and got back exhausted. Somewhere along the route, I bought a cool looking pair of sunglasses for twenty rupees. Meanwhile, the cooks had had the entire bogie to themselves. They had rested, relaxed and prepared dinner. All of us came back to a hearty Karnataka meal. That night, even the 5-year old snored like a 55-year old. I think we made the maximum noise ever, for a stationary bogie. Fortunately for Calcutta's rail passengers, we were placed far from the main platform.

The fun continued on the way back. Orissa wasn't very different in terms of weather, food or the kind of faces we saw on the streets. Konark Sun Temple was stunning. We had a guide who explained the science behind the three doorways (sunrays streaking through each during a particular season and falling on the deity), the wheels of the chariot that marked time, the huge magnet that was no longer there and the legend of the deity. On the way back, we passed by the Chandrabagha beach. The sand looked as pristine as Juhi Chawla and the water as blue as Lord Krishna. We were told that this was the most beautiful beach in India and readily believed it.

We reached Bangalore on May 20, 1988. We hugged and wept, wept and hugged, and wished each other good luck. I reached home the next day. A month and a half later, dad came back from work with a big steel plate in his hand, a very unusual sight. He told us that the Railways had some money left over from the trip, and therefore, had given a steel plate to the families of all the kids who had lived through the flood of sambar.

. . . .

(35)

POISONOUS GAS

It was a big year for all of us. We were in Class XII, technically called PUC 2nd year. The freewheeling existence of earlier years had been replaced by stress, ambition and competitiveness. Life had been taken over by classes, tuitions and revisions. My core gang of friends had turned into a studious, nervous bunch focused on the advancing exams.

Narasimha Murthy was highly intelligent but seemed to have gone off the earthly orbit. He spent an entire year without taking his eyes off the textbooks. Even while using the toilet, he ingested organic chemistry or calculus. He bathed neck downwards so that he could look at the textbook placed on a shelf nearby. His mom fed him breakfast while he solved complex physics problems. If we pushed him off a plane, theoretically of course, he would probably brush up on inorganic chemistry even as physics took him down. He had set very high hopes for himself and in the bargain, we had lost all hope of making eye contact with him through the year.

Arun Sharma was a brain of a different kind. He appeared cheerful all the time and was the first guy to walk out of an examination hall. Usually, he was also the first on the toppers' list. He was a brainy and goofy sort, but totally sorted.

Vishak Acharya was a grafter, more like Mike Brearley. He wasn't a whiz but not a dolt either. He always managed a decent score without ever setting anything on fire.

Deepak Shetty was a weak hand. Not losing-weak but

hoping-that-he-won't-lose weak. Academics stressed him out and he found solace in sports. Because of this, he read more sports magazines than textbooks. Somehow, he managed a decent inning each year.

I was a strange case. Since childhood, I had been Sunil Gavaskar in academics but in the past two years, turned into Srikanth. I didn't study much and cared even less. I could belt a few subjects and manage a more-than-decent seventy percent. I was pretty good at anything that didn't have formulae, equations, calculations, theorems or graphs. That left me with English and Biology.

When one combined all of us, we were a gang with intellectual sheen. A lot of students came to us for guidance. They mostly wanted net practice with Narasimha or Arun. Shetty and I were the gatekeepers. We guided people looking for guidance, about the opportune moment to approach Narasimha. He had gathered himself in so tight, that an ill-timed approach for help would shatter him into countless pieces. As was the practice, private tuitions in the evenings were taken far more seriously than the classrooms. Everyone attended them and so did we. One of the go-to lecturers was Viswanathaiyya. He was a stupendous teacher and most students went to him for Chemistry tuitions. The batches used to be mixed and students from different colleges came together. It was here that we first encountered Satisha. Till the tenth standard, he had studied in a Kannada medium school and had then swerved to an English medium college. To him, it was second life. He was a roguish looking chap, the sort I would have loved by my side in a street fight. In fact, a few days after we first met him, Satisha confided in me about his earlier existence. Here is a mild translation of what he told me:

"Anand, I was more into fights than studies. I used to regularly hit people, and no one had the guts to mess with me. But about a year ago, I woke up one day and wanted to score well and become a doctor. I don't know what came over me. Maybe I felt like tending to all the people I have pummelled."

He then laughed. He had his share of native wit. I was reminded of Valmiki, a man with a tumultuous past who had set foot on a path of self-redemption. My first interaction with him happened on the fourth day of tuitions.

Satisha: *Anand alva? Nim gang bagge baala kelidheeni.*

(Aren't you Anand? I have heard lots about your gang.)

I thanked him for his compliment and then he said,

Satisha: *Nim gang serbeku. Please neevella naninge help maadbeku!*

(I want to be part of your gang. All of you need to help me out, please!)

This was such a touching request. I assured him that we would do our best. After tuitions, I introduced him to the rest and told them about the deal. All of us felt for him. Narasimha didn't refuse but remarked with feeling,

Narasimha: *Aiyo! Nanige odhakke time illvalla...tch!*

(Oh Lord! I myself don't have time to study...tch!)

From that moment, Satisha became our ward. We went out of our way to help him learn. But he had a drawback, and a severe one at that. After ten years of studying in a Kannada medium school, it was a tall order to make rapid strides with English textbooks. So, I focused on improving his English. Narasimha, Arun and Vishak helped out in Physics, Chemistry and Maths. Shetty played an important role too. He boosted Satisha's confidence by repeatedly telling him that he would be a doctor. In the months leading up to the exams, I was amazed with his unwavering intent and desire. He was possessed and spent endless hours studying. In the evenings, he did a cycle tour of my house followed by Giddi's, Vishak's and Narasimha's. All the day's doubts across multiple subjects would be listed down. We would pick our respective topics and clarify things for him. After an hour or so, he would head back home and stay up till four in the morning.

Despite his resolve, his progress was far from encouraging. As the days passed, his eyes turned redder but he hadn't picked up much. We were puzzled by his lack of progress. Three months into this regimen, I decided to drop into his place one evening. I felt that maybe a personal visit would encourage him more. Giddi and I cycled across to Satisha's house, a mere ten minutes away. He was elated upon seeing us. We were taken aback upon seeing a large herd of cows in his house. His family ran a dairy business and had a healthy collection of cattle. Their house was obviously a much bigger size compared to ours, with a large compound. Satisha warmly took us inside to his decent-sized room. His table was littered with textbooks and numerous markers. This was a good sign. We sat down and slowly looked around as he disappeared inside to fetch water. We couldn't see an inch of the walls. Every part of every wall had been plastered with large chart papers. Every part of every chart paper had formulae written down, big and bold. When you combined Physics, Trigonometry, Calculus and Organic Chemistry, Class XII had more formulae than SBI branches in India. Because of this, Viswanathaiyya had told us a simple trick:

"Write down the important and difficult formulae across various subjects, on a sheet of paper. Paste it next to your bathroom mirror, or above your study table. Look at it several times a day as you go about your other chores. Trust me, they will get embedded in your brain."

This was a masterstroke of a suggestion and most of us had heeded his advice. But at most, we had a few A4 sheets pasted around in the house. Satisha had gone mental. He had copied every single formula from each subject. He had nearly replicated four textbooks and had spent innumerable man-hours doing so. Each wall, from the ceiling to the floor, had been dedicated to a particular subject. Needless to add, he hit a wall when it came to any of the subjects. He had been busy for months copying stuff from the textbooks onto the chart papers, and spent hardly any time understanding them. Finally, the redness in his eyes and the deadness in his mind made sense. We were now only a month away from the all-important public exams. I gave up my endeavour, cycled home in a tizzy and beseeched fate to take care of him.

His vain effort continued and pretty soon, the exams descended upon us. Satisha just wanted pass marks in all the papers. He had the benefit of a quota backing him. Most papers started with twenty objective type questions. All the just-pass candidates relied heavily on this. This was easier to cog and sometimes an ignorant tick would turn out right. If one somehow

managed to get a large part of this right, getting another 16-18 marks wasn't that difficult. And if one somehow managed 35, five grace marks came as a freebie. The aftermath of every paper always ended the same way. The shaky candidates would seek out the intelligent ones. Before they could forget what they had ticked inside, they would blurt out the answers and the Narasimhas of the world told them then and there, if they had got it right or not. Satisha always walked out to our gang. We had managed four papers and the next one was my department. The English question paper usually started with the grammar section:
1. Change from active voice to passive voice.
2. Who said the following to whom and when?
3. Verb patterns, noun phrases and clauses.

This was the equivalent of objective type questions before we moved onto those that needed elaborate answers. I breezed through the paper and walked out fairly early, having done more-than-fairly well. The final bell rang thrice, and the crowd walked out with Satisha among them, looking quite pleased. Our gang huddled together and this time, I did the enquiry. Satisha kept smiling and nodding his head, meaning that he had it covered. For all the effort I had put into him, I wanted his answers, not his confidence. I went question by question. In the `Change from active to passive' section, the second poser was: *The poisonous gas killed 350 people.* Satisha said that this was a sitter. I pressed him for his answer.

Satisha: *350 people killed the poisonous gas.*

Months later, after the public exam and Entrance Test results were out, Satisha was ranked about 12,000. He got a medical seat in one of the colleges in Karnataka. A year later, he decided that medicine wasn't fit for him, and dropped out. He joined the reputed National Institute of Engineering in Mysore, and became the secretary of the Students' Union.

. . . .

(36)

DEATH WISH

Every now and then, a slightly bizarre streak cropped up in me. It started early on, and continued to strike me every few years. Each time, it compelled me to push the boundaries of human endeavour. This was my Olympics.

In the third standard, I had picked up a new vocation, drawing comic characters. On Sundays, I spent hours copying them from comic books. I found it easy to draw any picture that had a strong outline, and regularly drew Mickey Mouse, Goofy, Uncle Donald and the rest. The size, proportions and expressions used to turn out quite well. Soon, my friends in class started calling me an artist. Because, hearing this felt so good, I drew more. I didn't have money for sketch pens and some of the richer friends used to lend me their sets. Sometimes, I coloured my drawings in the time between classes. Once the masterpiece was done, I gifted it to whoever had booked it first. All in all, life was wonderful and I had no compulsion to make social impressions. But strangely, being good at one thing told me that I could do something else too. It pushed me to try things beyond the ordinary. Like, hitting a six off the last ball was big but boring; it had to be at least nine runs. I had to make people gasp. And so, one day, just for a lark, just before the start of the final period, I told a few friends that I would eat a piece of blade. There was pure shock and excitement. I hadn't done this before. In fact, it had never crossed my mind even remotely. Impetuously, I had thought up this big circus act and now they couldn't wait to witness it. I decided on a private show and only 5-6 close friends were informed. The legend had to spread.

The final bell rang, and the class dispersed quickly. The invitees gathered around my desk. I had already pulled out the blade from my geometry box. As tense faces stared, I pressed one corner of the blade onto the desk, till it snapped. The tiny piece was the smallest triangle I had seen till then. I held it up for everyone and placed it on my left molar. Everyone's mouth was open wider than mine. I brought down my upper teeth and started gnashing it. I clenched my jaws hard and didn't let it drop next to my gums. After removing the sharpness off the edges, I got it onto my tongue and displayed it to six open mouths. I then took it to the other side and chewed hard for a minute more. It was mangled and I sent it down the gullet. I opened my mouth wide, pulled down my lower lip, stretched my cheeks and bared my gums all around. There was stunned silence followed by big looks of appreciation and admiration. One of them called me Tarzan. Of course, Tarzan had never eaten blades, but I got the point. The `shock & awe' show was over. I headed home without any worrisome possibilities in my head. The next morning, I was fine.

This became a weekly feature. After the 5th or the 6th swallowing, the stunt lost its sheen. People did look forward to it but the outcome was known; the piece of blade always succumbed. So, I decided to try something a little more interactive. I thought for a while and zeroed in on pinching. The convent had a series of punishments for a series of offences. Pinching was a regular punishment for talking during class, not doing homework, not knowing the right answer, mis-spelling a word, having a shirt button open, not wearing one's house badge, forgetting to carry one's homework book, having untied laces, wearing two ribbons of different shades, having ink stains on clothes, not dotting the `j' or the `i', not bringing up the tail of the `g', and having blackberry stains on our teeth. Pinching had two forms and qualified well for `Shock & Awe: Part 2'. Sometimes, the teachers would pinch the softer, fairer, inner part of our forearms or the back of our thighs with their finger joints. This was a `Yowww!' kind of pain. At other times, they literally skinned our earlobes or forearms with their long nails. This was the `Aiyeeeeeeeeee!' kind. I announced to the core gang that the coming week, I would swallow a small piece of blade and then, hold out my arms for a minute. All of them could pinch me simultaneously with all their might. They could use their phalanges and nails. In fact, I urged them to start growing their nails. I wasn't anywhere near being the strongest in class. There were some real tough guys: Avinash, Shirish, Sai Charan, Meghraj and the two Muzammils. One of them was called Mudguard, a sobriquet he had earned since he was the first person in our class to remove the mudguards from his cycle. The other was Gun House Muzzamil, as his family owned one. My most coveted gift was a bullet pendant that he had given me. It was also the most stress-causing gift. While all of them were much stronger, the spirit behind what came into my head was stronger than theirs. So, the next week, after the boring ritual of chewing up a tiny piece of blade, I held out my hands. Six people looked at me for one last moment of bravado and permission. The next instant, there were twelve sets of fingers going berserk. With every ounce of strength, they twisted my skin, cut into it with their nails, pulling out little millimeters of it, hung from it with their body weight and tried just about everything. I didn't withdraw my hands or wince. The skin on my forearm came apart in many places. The pain was killing me but it was mind over matter. I goaded them to perform better. After a minute, all of us stopped gracefully. This continued for a few weeks after which, this too became passable.

I then introduced the third act: punching. After the blade and the pinching, I would hold my breath, harden my stomach and stand with my feet slightly apart. All of them got two punches at my stomach, a total of twelve for me. I was most apprehensive about this compared to the other two dares. All of them tried their best to dissuade me. I mocked their lack of guts to the point where they started readying their fists. Avinash's fist looked like a cork ball, both in size and colour. As he was about to land a punch,

I told him not to hit me too hard, for his own benefit. He paused, looking bemused. I said that if he went through my stomach wall, the blade pieces inside would cut up his fist. I laughed nervously while he took a breath and increased the breadth of his fist. Now, it wasn't clenched so hard. He still crosschecked if I was sure. I nodded and he punched. The rest followed. They altered the sequence for the second set. The punches were hard but I survived. All of us looked spent. I felt that none of them had used his full strength. I said that they were all in the region of 70%, a good score but way below what they were capable of. We picked up our bags and walked out of school. Before heading in various directions, they hugged me with concern and gently patted my stomach.

Eating blades, getting pinched, and getting punched in the stomach carried on for a few more weeks. I never screamed in pain. No one broke his fist. Nothing big happened, other than one of them getting an ear-pinch from Emilia Miss for growing his nails too long. Soon after, I stopped these acts as unexpectedly as they had begun. Years passed, and this became a distant memory. One day, when I was in the 7th standard, I suddenly remembered these silly acts and told mom in passing that I used to eat blades. She slapped me so hard that it hurt more than all the pinches and the punches. That's only because I hadn't braced myself for it. She screamed at me saying that if I ever tried it again, she would slit my throat with a blade. And then she broke down uncontrollably. I calmed her, saying it was a thing of the past; four years had gone by and nothing had happened. She continued to weep.

Life rolled on with other interesting pursuits, and I was now in PUC 2nd year, big and worldly-wise. On a Sunday, I was at Ramu's house, along with Compti and Sudeep, whiling away time. He went into the kitchen, chopped up a couple of cucumbers, sprinkled salt and chilli powder, and came out with a plate of salad. He also carried two steel bowls, with salt and chilli powder, in case someone wanted more of these. Ramu lived in a large joint family, and the kitchen was larger than an Ashok Leyland truck. Everything was stored in big quantities. The steel bowls were filled to the brim. We continued chatting and enjoying the salad, when Ramu addressed me specifically,

Ramu: *Dabba, ee butlu mensin pudi thinnak aagatha?*

(Can you eat this bowl of chilli powder?)

Nonchalantly, I replied that it wasn't a big deal. The rules hadn't been laid down, or the stakes decided. It was a random question, and I had uttered a random and defiant response. Since it was dismissed as easily doable, all of us started thinking. We kept looking at each other to see if we were really serious, and whether this randomness was worth pursuing. Ramu added that the entire bowl had to be finished in one shot; that I couldn't have it in spoonfuls. And if I did manage, I couldn't drink water for five minutes after that.

Me: *Eshtu?*

(How much?)

Ramu said, 'Ten rupees'. This was incidental and irrelevant. The point wasn't about winning or losing money. It was about either winning or losing in a random act. Something like this had never been attempted, and I was compelled to give it a shot. In less than three minutes, boyhood banter had turned serious. Four of us sat around the table, with the bowl of chilli powder in the centre. Without even thinking, I upturned the bowl into my mouth. Contrary to what all of us believed, Agni didn't strike. Instead, Lord Hanuman took over. My mouth was stretched to its maximum. I had packed myself with so much dry powder that I couldn't breathe. There wasn't any scope for my mouth to generate saliva. I had a logjam. Nearly a minute passed, and I hadn't managed to swallow even a pinch of it. I stood and tilted my head up. My jaws started aching, and so did my neck. I thought I would die if it remained stuck like this. But I didn't want to give up. The three of them were rolling with laughter and calling me Chilli Powder Hanuman. Ever so slowly, with immense difficulty, I managed to push tiny quantities of chilli powder down my throat. Once a sane quantity went down, the task became easy. My mouth had room to manoeuvre. I started generating saliva and quickly took in the rest. It had been an ordeal for 2-3 minutes but I won. The victory tasted exquisite. Ramu, Compti and Sudeep stared at me as if I had swallowed an anaconda. With my eyes the colour of chilli powder, I managed to smile. They were expecting me to start screaming in agony any minute. Surprisingly, my mouth wasn't on fire. I did feel the spice, but it was well within limits. Ramu picked up the glass of water from the table and held it away from me. To make a bigger show, I started whistling a Dr.Rajkumar tune: *ninade nenapu dinavu manadalli*…Five minutes passed before Ramu offered me the glass. I didn't drink it for the next half an hour. The next morning, there was zero torment.

A few months later, Compti arrived with great news. His family had signed up as bottlers for Torino and Dixi Cola, two popular soft drinks in the South. They had started work on the plant, which was 10-12 kilometres outside of Shimoga. A bottle of soft drink didn't mean the world to us, but the fact that we had our own plant and could drink at will, made it extraordinarily special. Soon, the plant was operational. On a Sunday afternoon, five of us got into Compti's Maruti 800 and headed there. It was a beautiful place spread over a few acres. The plant sat in the middle and had lush green lawns all around. We were taken on a tour of the facility. We had never seen soft drinks being bottled before, and the assembly line gliding past with its bottles, looked amazing. Two of us decided to count the number of bottles and ended up very confused after a while. This reminded me of what Sriram and I used to do as kids. Every time we travelled by train and crossed another, we tried counting the number of bogies. We rarely got it right. The toughest was when we happened to cross VaiGai Express. This train ran across Tamilnadu and was one of the fastest then.

After our little tour, we walked out and sat in a circle on the lawns. It was consumption time. From the moment we had left Shimoga, I had repeatedly told Compti that I would have 20-30 bottles. Compti had countered each time by asking me to clear out the entire plant. A couple of workers walked up to us with two trays of Torino and Dixi Cola. We were five and each tray held twelve. The plant bottled only 300 ml bottles. With so much orange and black in front of us, I rubbed my palms in glee. I knocked back a Dixi, then a Torino, another Dixi, yet another, one more Torino and rounded it off with a Dixi. Compti kept telling me to go easy. But this was more greed and less randomness. After the first three bottles, my gulps had become smaller and less frenetic but somehow, I managed to drink up six 300 ml bottles in less than ten minutes. Everyone else was on his third. I let out a series of burps averaging more than 3.8 per bottle. I then leaned back on my elbows and smiled in satisfaction.

Within a minute, I started feeling horribly funny. I felt like I was about to deliver a large litter. My stomach felt obscenely bloated. I started sweating profusely and experienced total breathlessness. My face turned red, a mix of Torino and Dixi colours. Gasping badly, I groaned and lay down while everyone kept laughing. I was prone to theatrics of this kind. I had done edgier things like blades and chilli powder, and so tried telling myself that this can't go bad. But I swear I had never felt this sick ever. I tried taking in big gasps of air but couldn't breathe. With great effort, I managed to lie on my side but felt no better. I went back on my back again and for once in my life, started calling out to a doctor seriously. They thought I was still joking but pretty soon realized that I was close to death. The panic must have shown on my face. The nearest doctor was 12 kilometres away in Shimoga. Compti suggested that we rush there immediately. I whispered that they should fetch the doctor as I could hardly move. Someone ran inside and got the manager and a couple of workers. One of them put his hand on my stomach and was about to press down when I somehow managed to yell him off me. As home remedies and bottling plant remedies were being discussed, I let out a long burp. For the first time in 18 minutes, I managed to breathe clearly once. I lay there gasping and moaning for a long time with seven faces peering down. They kept dabbing the sweat on my forehead. One kept squeezing my palm gently. Inch by inch, minute by minute, burp by burp, breath by breath, I felt better and better. I had been in the Death Zone for 45 minutes.

Of the three heroic attempts, this was the worst, by a long mile. Perhaps, age had started catching up with me.

. . . .

(37)

COMFFFORTABLY DUMB

I had finished my first year BBM at ATNCC (Acharya Tulsi National College of Commerce), Shimoga. It was April 1991 and in August, dad would turn 58 and retire, whether he liked it or not. We decided to move to Mysore, after 26 years in Shimoga. Dad had grown up there and it was a natural choice. It was also a retiree's paradise, besides being a great place for education. Some of its other draws were terrific weather, low cost of living and proximity to Bangalore. Since my second year started in May, I had to move in advance and enrol in a college in Mysore.

God must have been in one of his most generous moods. Around the same time, Deepak Shetty's family also decided to shift to Mysore. It had nothing to do with our decision. His father owned a coffee estate near Chikmaglur. He felt that being in Mysore made more sense in order to manage the estate. Deepak and I had been thick friends since Class VIII and his parents treated me like their son. In fact, many a time, they would embarrass me by extending more privileges than they normally did within their own family. Deepak, one of my closest buddies, also behaved in a similar fashion. It was truly karmic. Both families were overjoyed. His parents bought a 3-bedroom house in Kuvempunagar and I stayed with them for a few months.

Deepak and I got admission in Basudev Somani College, less than half a kilometre from his house. Every second weekend, I would visit home. Strangely, I had started disliking trains and preferred bus journeys, though they were many times more cumbersome. These were the red KSRTC buses, most of which were also nearing retirement age, just like dad. My parents never got this. Dad would always ask me, stressing his 'f' like he always did,

Dad: *Ananda, comfffortable aagi train alli barod bittu adyako vadhaad kondu bus alli barthya?*

(Instead of travelling comfffortably by train, why do you suffer and come by bus?)

So, on one particular trip, I decided to heed dad's suggestion. He came up with a sensible plan. Towards the fag end of his career, he had graduated to a passenger train guard and plied between Shimoga and Bangalore. Dad's train would leave Bangalore at 9 pm and reach Shimoga at 6 am. At 1 am, it reached the midpoint, Arasikere Junction. The Hubli Mail left Mysore at 7 pm and reached Arasikere Junction at 12:20 am.

Dad: *Ananda, take the Hubli Mail and wait for my train. Then, sleep comfffortably in the first-class compartment.*

I reached Arasikere as scheduled. I put my head on the kit bag and lay down on a platform bench waiting for dad's train. His train pulled in on the dot. Wearily, I got up to see that dad had walked up to me. The first-class compartment had stopped a short distance from where I was. The coach was empty. It had four compartments and a coupé, and not a single berth was occupied. The only occupant was the Coach Attendant. He was in a blue blazer and looked like a TTE. A Coach Attendant was like an executive to tend to the privileged first-class commuters. This was a recent thing prevalent on trains that plied from and to big cities. As the three of us stood there, I knew exactly what dad would tell him, and he didn't prove me wrong.

Dad: *Ivru num kade avru. Ondu berth kotbidi.*

(This personage is from our side. Please provide him a berth.)

Dad was the main guard and the authority on the train. He didn't need to request the Coach Attendant, rather, just command him. On top of that, the coach was empty, and the person in question was his son, not some bloody personage. Rather than get annoyed, I smiled to myself. I had seen too many years of dad by now. He was made of X and Y chromosomes, like any of us, except that his X was called Gandhi and Y, Siddhartha. The Coach Attendant belonged to the changing breed like me, whose genes had started mutating. He didn't even hear out the request. To him, I was clearly the guard's son or nephew, and before dad could finish his sentence, he retorted,

CA: *Yenu thondre illa saar. Neevu dayavittu hogi.*

(Sir, not at all an issue. You please carry on.)

As dad walked back to the end of the train, I jumped in and entered the first compartment with four vacant berths. I put my kit bag on the upper berth and was about to go up. The train began to move. The Coach Attendant bolted the main bogie door and walked in.

CA: *Mel yaak hogthidheeri? Kelgade malkondbidi, comfffortable aagi.*

(Why are you going up? Sleep below, comfffortably.)

It wasn't just dad. Most Kannadigas in the railways stressed on the 'f'.

The lower berth was obviously more comfortable as it had a wider backrest that could be pulled down. I shoved my kit bag underneath and lay down. Since we were travelling first-class, it came with pillows and bed sheets. Within minutes, I was drifting off to sleep. He lingered around for a bit, slid the compartment door shut and then lay down next to me. In my stupor, I vaguely thought that this was strange as there were three vacant berths. But honestly, I was too sleepy to react. I had consumed two bottles of Kingfisher before boarding. In a fatherly, caring voice, he asked me to take off my jacket. I mumbled that I was feeling cold. He suggested that we could cover ourselves with the bed sheet and did so. He then placed his hand on my chest. My mind stirred. Still half-asleep, I started wondering what to do. I was neither so comfortable nor so dumb to not realize that I was between a wall and a hard place. But on this night, there were two inner forces that made me react slowly. One was my beer-drowsiness. The other was a mind frozen with discomfort. I just didn't know how to react. It's not that I was alarmed or scared. I was just, `Huh?'

[Later on, a lot of my friends told me that I should have punched him. They said that in my position, they would have beaten him to pulp. Some even teased me that I didn't have the balls. That's not true. As I grew up, I grew highly reluctant towards violence, of any kind or degree. Force and fierceness became my pet peeves. I found them pointless and disturbing, even towards a right cause or in defence. My tendency was to walk away from such situations.]

I sat up. He asked me if anything was wrong. I mumbled that I needed to go to the toilet. Once inside, I contemplated my next step. One option was to threaten him and then lie down in the adjoining compartment. The other was to get off the coach and go to dad's cabin. I imagined trying to explain to dad, the reason for joining him in the middle of the night. But I was so sure that dad would not understand what a gay man meant. I found this quite funny and let out a small laugh. It was best that dad didn't hear about this at all. I felt the sanest option was to get off this bogie and jump into another. So, I stood in the toilet waiting for the train to reach the next station. It must have been about four minutes and the CA came knocking on the door.

CA: *Hello! All ok?*

I replied that I was fine and would join him soon. There was neither annoyance nor panic in my voice. I was sure he had been worried sick in the past four minutes: would I barge out and smash him with the cistern? Or had I decided to kill myself? My voice assured him and he went inside the compartment.

At this moment, the train creaked to a halt. From inside the toilet, I could make out nothing but was sure we had reached the next station. I bolted out of the toilet, unlatched the main door and was about to jump on the platform when I shrank back. We were in the midst of nowhere. The train had halted and was waiting for the signal. It stood on a bund, about ten feet high. As I carefully stepped down on the sloping bund, the train whistled and moved. I quickly jumped onto the steps of the next bogie and held the vertical iron bars on the sides of the door. After steadying myself, I gripped the bar tightly with my left hand and started banging the door with my right. A train door is 2-3 inches thick and this one was locked from inside. The train gathered speed and was hurtling. After banging the door repeatedly for 3-4 minutes, someone opened it. He turned out to be a beggar who had been lying next to it. This was the general compartment, and it was carrying 2.5 times its capacity. Every inch of the bogie had been taken and there were people lying all over the floor - beggars, underprivileged vendors and pitiable old villagers. After shutting the door, I had place for one foot. I stood there like a stork, leaned back into the corner and travelled the rest of the night like this. Every quarter of an hour, I alternated my legs. It turned out to be the longest half-night of my life. My mind was more numb than my feet. It went through some indistinct plans of rounding up a few railway quarters' friends and giving the CA a hiding.

At 6:10 am, the train pulled into Shimoga Town. I hopped off and went next door, as my kit bag was still there. The Coach Attendant looked fresh from a night of undisturbed sleep. He casually asked me where I had disappeared. I casually told him that I had chanced upon a friend in the adjoining bogie. Twenty minutes later, dad signed off and both of us walked home.

Dad: *Wasn't it comfffortable?*

Me: *Totttally dad!*

He smiled and remarked that there was good reason he always insisted that I take the train.

. . . .

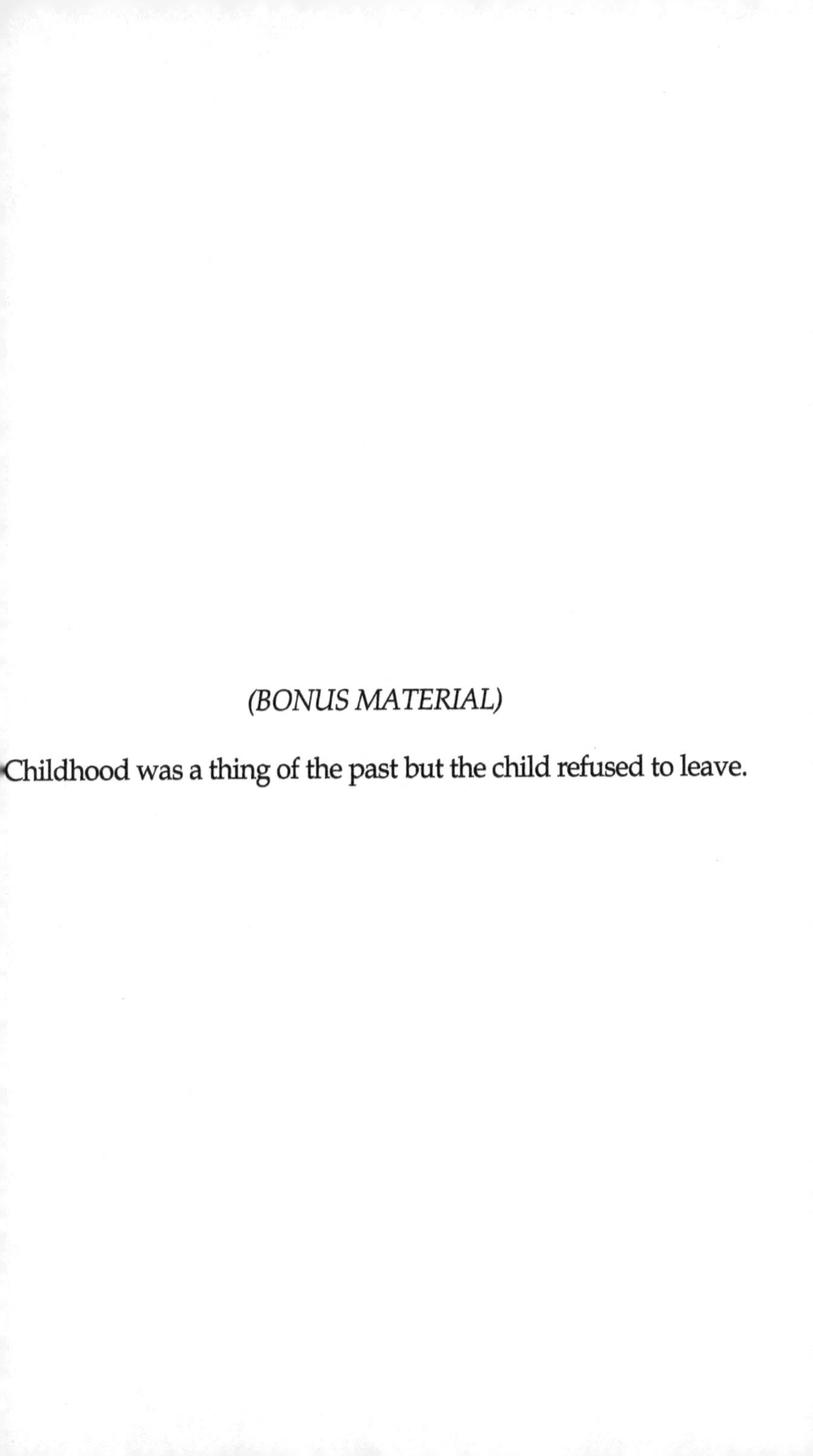

(BONUS MATERIAL)

Childhood was a thing of the past but the child refused to leave.

(38)

THE GREATEST EXCHANGE

1996. I had done a year in Mudra and had started gaining respect from peers and seniors. I had a long way to go, had lots more to prove but it was apparent that I was cut out for the business of advertising. That's what mattered the most to me. I was in a happy space, got promoted and my monthly salary stood at Rs.7800. It was a decent sum but barely sufficient to live in Bombay, especially when one was a migrant. But the future looked bright, and I lived somewhat beyond my means, largely due to a Citibank and a Standard Chartered credit card. I had a combined credit limit of Rs.15,000.

A year had passed since I had visited home. Finally, I managed to take a couple of weeks off. On my 24-hour bus journey from Bombay to Bangalore, I actively thought of home and parents for the first time in a year. Despite all my indifference and our differences of opinion, I loved mom and dad dearly. The only painful knot in my heart was that, in all these years, I had bought them nothing. This wasn't entirely my fault. When I had got my first paycheck, I had wanted to buy a sari for mom and a shirt for dad; not because I was in a 1950s movie or that I couldn't think of anything else. It was just that anything else would've been wasted on them. They used so little in their lives. And if I ever bought them anything without informing them first, they would lie awake in bed for three days distressing over the wasted amount. Therefore, I had informed them about my intended purchase.

Dad: *I have 4 first-class shirts. Dhuddu waste maadbeda, save maadko.*

(I have 4 first-class shirts. Don't waste money, save it for yourself.)

Mom: *Iro seere-ne udalla. Dhuddu waste maadbeda.*

(I don't wear the sarees I have. Don't waste money on another.)

I had cursed them in my mind for their frugality and hadn't made the purchases. But now, there was a golden opportunity, one they couldn't dismiss as wasting money. In my eyes, they had become old. Sriram had moved to Tokyo and was working with Honeywell. After a few years in Mysore, mom and dad had shifted to Bangalore since this was more central, and a lot of our relatives resided there. They lived happily, in a small rented house in Jayanagar 9th Block. A maidservant came for 20 minutes in the mornings to sweep and swab the house. She didn't do the utensils or wash clothes because mom and dad had decided that they could handle these. And we didn't have a washing machine. I noticed this gap in their lives and was thrilled with my discovery. This was a useful, needed and fantastic investment, even by their measure. Beyond all, this would make me guilt-free for the next five years at least. A semi-automatic cost about twelve thousand. I hadn't saved but had sufficient credit on my cards. I couldn't wait to reach home.

The next morning, I was home by eight. The bus ride had been bumpy and I had hardly slept. Yet, I was as wide awake as a first-time prisoner. After breakfast and coffee, the three of us sat around while I told them about Bombay, Mudra, my PG mates etc. After dispensing with these topics, I asked dad what his plan of action for the day was. He said that he had nothing lined up. I smiled. Feeling like a wealthy benefactor, I announced,

Me: *Appa, ready aagi. 4th Block Complex-ge hogona.*

(Dad, get ready. Let's go to the 4th Block Complex.)

He asked me what was going on there.

Me: *Justu. Manege ondhu washing machine tharona.*

(Just. Let's get a washing machine for the house.)

I had deliberately added `Just' at the beginning to make it seem like a trivial purchase.

Dad: *Washing machine-a? Yarige?*

(Washing machine? For whom?)

This was deliberate ignorance and so I ignored it. Dad took his time.

Dad: *Washing machine-ge dhuddu save maadidhya?*

(Have you saved money for a washing machine?)

I nodded. He asked me to show him my passbook. I sighed. The old man had started drawing me into a trap.

Me: *Appa, passbook illa, dhuddu idhe. Banni hogona.*

(Dad, there's no passbook but there's money. Let's go.)

His Gandhian smile crossed his face.

Dad: *I am happy you are thinking of us. Ashte saaku, innenu beda.*

(I am happy you are thinking of us. That's enough, need nothing else.)

I brushed aside his middle-class sentiment and said that they needed a washing machine. Dad drew a deep breath. He painstakingly explained that he had to wash just one shirt, one banian, and one underwear every day; and that when he went for his bath, he managed this easily. A similar routine applied to mom as well. He then thanked God for keeping their limbs strong and said that they didn't need a washing machine for a few more years.

Dad: *Dhuddu waste maadbeda, save maadko.*

(Don't waste money, save it for yourself.)

For 24 years of my life, every conversation was only around money, discussed in the most sensible way, of course. But there was so much of life beyond money. There were matters of necessity, of a little indulgence, of a son's pride, of wanting to pamper them etc. And on this trip, nothing had consumed me more than seeing a washing machine at home, and seeing my credit card debited. I exploded,

Me: *Dhuddu! Waste-oo! Save-oo! Idhu bitre life ye illa!*

(Money! Waste! Save! Apart from this, there's no life!)

I then barked that I was heading out and buying the washing machine. Dad gathered his maximum resolve and said that he would never use it. He was enormously capable of such a stupid act. Without raising a hand, he had punched me so hard that my eyes were swollen and shut tight. I had to throw in the towel. He got up and headed out to buy groceries. I cursed and cursed, silently, of course. I cursed their common sense, contentment, good nature and steadfastness. I ranted in my head that they deserved to suffer. I prayed that they should wash their clothes well into their nineties. Suddenly, I was alarmed at my amount of ill will towards them and felt guilty. I calmed down a bit and focused on my own life. It looked screwed up. On the very first day itself, my Bangalore trip had been ruined beyond repair. Feeling helpless, I switched on ESPN. Lunch happened along with some middle-class conversation. In the evening, I headed to MG Road to meet up with my friends. My routine had been the same for years since college. I would spend the day at home, head out in the evening, sleep over at some friend's house and come back the next morning. I had developed night allergy to my house since nightlife at home was as exciting as Doordarshan. Today was no different. I had been back after a year and a large bunch of friends were meeting up. At the end of the night, I slept at Sandeep Shenoy's place, which overlooked the golf course.

I woke up at eight, hailed an auto and headed home. While passing through Gandhi Bazaar, I saw a big departmental store. I was familiar with these large format stores in Bombay, and they had just started making an appearance in Bangalore. I asked the auto driver to stop, paid him and got off. As I walked in, my head was filled with a series of emphatic statements: I wasn't allowed to buy a washing machine, but I could definitely buy things for the house! Dad, and even his dad, could have no arguments against that! I took a shopping cart and ambled down the aisle. Picturing the house in my head, I started making notes of things that were used or consumed. I started with the bathroom and went to the toiletries section. Dad used to shave every morning, come light or darkness. His razor had served him for 35 years and was still going strong. So, I picked up shaving cream. I moved on to soaps, toothpastes, shampoos and detergents. Beyond these, the bathroom held nothing. Shampoo too was a very recent addition. Mom had made her shampoo-debut at the age of 58. Sriram had got a bottle on his first trip back from Tokyo and she used it every now and then. When I was done, my cart looked colourful and cheerful.

Godrej Shaving Cream (4)
Colgate (1), Pepsodent (1), Promise (1), Close Up (1)
Lifebuoy (2), Lux (2), Medimix (2), Hamam (2),
Cinthol (2), Godrej Shikakai (2), Mysore Sandal (2)
Clinic (1), Pantene (1), Nyle (1), Chik (1), Sunsilk (1)
Rin (6)

The bathroom was taken care of. I then thought of the dressing table and picked up a few things.

Parachute (2), Dabur Amla (1), Coco Raj (1), Nihar (1)
Ponds (1), Cuticura (1), Cinthol (1), Nycil (1)
Fair & Lovely (2), Ponds Cold Cream (2),
Vicco Turmeric (2), Nivea (2)

As my mind moved from the dressing table towards the kitchen, it stopped abruptly. Just outside the kitchen was the refrigerator and I recollected its contents. All through my growing up years, we had never been big on butter and jam. But the world had changed, and so had mom and dad, in this department. Now, they bought and consumed butter and jam in small quantities. Once a week, mom felt that it wasn't worth making breakfast for just the two of them. On such days, they had two slices of bread with a little jam and butter. HLL and Amul had finally cracked the Subbarao kitchen. Along with these, other items had also slipped in, an odd bottle of squash and a few bars of Cadbury's chocolates.

Amul Butter – 100g (6)
Kissan Jam – 100g (Mixed Fruit, Pineapple, Strawberry, Orange)
Kissan Squash – 250g (Orange, Mango, Pineapple)
Cadbury Dairy Milk (10 big bars)

I was done with the fridge and moved to the kitchen, in my head.
Mysore Sanna Rice (10 kg)

Toor Dal (5 kg)
Urad Dal (2 kg)
Moong Dal (2 kg)
Atta (5 kg)
Sugar (5 kg)
Jaggery (4 kg)
Poha (3 kg)
Rava (3 kg)
Sundrop Cooking Oil (5 packets)
Ghee (1 kg)
Red Chillies (1 kg)
Tamarind (3 kg)
Filter Coffee Powder (3 kg)
Brooke Bond Red Label (2 kg), Agni (2 kg), Kannan Devan (2 kg)
Chilli Powder (500g), Turmeric Powder (500g), Mustard (500g)
Groundnuts (3 kg)
Asafoetida (3 packets)
Cut mango pickle (1), vadu manga (1), lime (1)

I checked my head for any omissions. Everything was covered. The pile was so high that it threatened to topple. I pushed the cart as carefully as people play jenga. Twenty-five minutes later, I saw the longest bill of my life. I held it at my shoulder, and it stopped just above my ankle. The total was Rs.4,830. I handed over my StanChart credit card. As he swiped it, I gurgled like a baby. It was one of my most gratifying `spending' acts. I hailed an auto, and the attendant helped me with the loading. I barely had place to sit. When I reached home, it was close to ten. Dad and mom had gone out, most likely to the bank. I arranged all the stuff on our dining table (the same one that had figured in the epic sambar fight). When I was done, it looked like a small shop with countless shapes, colours and packaging. Feeling vindicated, I switched on the TV and sat down.

Forty minutes later, dad and mom returned. As dad stepped in, he changed from active to passive and froze like a snowman. His pupils had dilated to the maximum, and he didn't blink for the next 130 seconds. Slowly, with utmost difficulty, he rediscovered his speech.

Dad: *Ananda, yenappa idhu!*

(What is this!)

I casually replied that I had bought stuff for the house and nothing more. He tottered and sat down. By now, even you will know his next question.

Dad: *Yeshtu kharch maadidhya?*

(How much have you spent?)

I refused and said that it didn't matter. He insisted a second time and I looked away. He asked me to produce the bill.

Me: *No dad. Nothing doing!*

['Nothing doing!' was a phrase that he had used extensively on me in my growing up years - when I had wanted to learn drums and karate, wanted my first pair of stone wash jeans, wanted to skip a puja, keep a dog, grow my hair etc.]

Now I dealt back the same phrase. He locked his eyes with mine. I stared back at him without blinking. Realization slowly seeped into him that he was locking horns with an advertising professional from Bombay, and not his obedient, little boy in stretchlon shorts. After gathering his equilibrium, he stated that he didn't need the bill. Pulling out his little diary and a pen, he proceeded towards the dining table muttering that most packs had MRPs on them and he could calculate. As for the kitchen items, he stated that he had more than a fair estimate of what they cost. It was just impossible to beat him in a game of stupid wits. Now, I was on the back foot. This exercise would take him an hour, at the very least. I jumped and pulled out the bill. He saw the length and shrank in size. Both were of a similar height now. He sat down on the divan and stared at each item in silence, for the next eight minutes. Then, and I swear on my ancestors, he wailed and whimpered.

Dad: *Aiyo! Helkolakke naachike aagatha! Nan maga MBA but ondhu paisa buddhi ilvalla antha.*

(Alas! I am ashamed! I am ashamed to tell the world that my son is an MBA, but doesn't have one paisa of intelligence.)

He hung his head in shame, shook it slowly and hung it again. He then got up, went to the table and picked up a tube of shaving cream.

Dad: *Ananda, I am happy that you are thinking of us. But little common sense you should have, no? We are two people. How much shaving cream will I use? How much jam will we consume? We can't eat toothpaste, right? If you wanted to buy things, I can understand one toothpaste, one shaving cream, one jam…but four four, five five? So unnecessary and a total waste of money. These shaving creams will last for two years, at least.*

He then picked up every item and made an individual comment about how long each was going to last.

Shaving Cream (2 years)

Toothpaste (2.5 years)

Soap (6 months)

Shampoo (7 years)

Detergent Bar (4 months)

Coconut Oil (1 year 2 months)

Talcum Powder (1 year)

Cream (11 months)

Butter (1.4 years)

Jam (2 years)

Squash (2.5 years)

Chocolate (6 to 7 months)

I was amazed at his precision. He wasn't done yet. There was a different angle to the kitchen items.

Dad: *Kitchen items, we consume daily but still, how much? Some of the items are wokay, but some are a waste. Rava and dal will get worms. Red chillies will lose their pungency. Plus, there is no place in the kitchen to keep all these. Let me tell you one more thing. On the first of every month, I go to the shop at the corner. I bring first-class rice, first-class dal and everything else, at reasonable prices. If you had bought all these things there, you would have cent percent saved at least 800 rupees. You have no value for money!*

Hoooofffff! Both of us let out a similar, long breath for totally different reasons. But he had a point. I had been too sentimental and foolish. Dad plopped down heavily on the divan. After five minutes, he stood upright and said,

Dad: *Ananda, I can only think of one thing. We can somehow make use of the kitchen items. We can prepare more during festivals and distribute. All other items, we will keep one one unit. The remaining, let's go and exchange for kitchen items.*

I stared at him in a way I had never stared at anyone before.

Me: *Appa, adhu dhodda departmental store. Exchange maadalla, baidhu vapas kalasthaare.*

(Dad, it's a big departmental store. They won't exchange but curse and send us back.)

I honestly believed so. Dad's mission sounded more childish than my act.

Dad: *Departmental...mental alla thane? Bill idhe. We are not asking for money back. We are only exchanging items.*

(Departmental...not mental, right? We have the bill. We are not asking for money back. We are only exchanging items.)

I tried my best to convince him. After what I had put him through, I didn't want dad to be humiliated in public. I refused to get up. He waited for two minutes, strode out and came back with an auto. He picked sixty percent of the items and loaded them. I was so shocked that I didn't even get up to help him.

An hour later, I heard the sound of an auto. This time, I ran out. Dad had managed the exchange. He had come back with more jaggery, sugar, oil, groundnuts, tamarind, rice, dal etc. I was astounded and felt great admiration for him. I didn't let him lift a single packet. As he paid the auto guy, I ferried all of it. Dad walked in looking a lot relaxed.

Dad: *Embatthu rupay auto-ge bere waste aaythu.*

(Wasted 80 rupees on the auto also.)

He said it matter-of-factly, not as a barb. As mom got busy arranging over a hundred packets in the kitchen, I honestly wanted to know how dad had managed this.

Dad: *Nothing at all! I told them that my most foolish son had come in the morning and had bought most foolish items. They said it was wokay to exchange. Decent people.*

We then sat down for lunch.

· · · · · · · ● ● ● ● ● ● · · · · · · · ·

FOR YOUR OWN
`HALF PANTS FULL PANTS'
MEMORIES

FOR YOUR OWN
`HALF PANTS FULL PANTS'
MEMORIES

FOR YOUR OWN
`HALF PANTS FULL PANTS'
MEMORIES

Anand Subbarao (also known as Anand Suspi)
has been an advertising writer for nearly 25 years.

Half Pants Full Pants is his debut novel,
a childhood memoir, that was first published in 2016.

In 2022, it was adapted into a web series.

asuspi@gmail.com   Anand Suspi